ART, THE ART COMMUNITY, AND THE LAW

ART, THE ART COMMUNITY, AND THE LAW

A legal and business guide for artists, collectors, gallery owners, and curators

Edited by
Stephen B. Smart, LL.B.
with Mary Baxter

Self-Counsel Press
(a division of)
International Self-Counsel Press Ltd.
Canada U.S.A.

Printed in Canada

First edition: June, 1994

Canadian Cataloguing in Publication Data

Main entry under title:
Art, the art community, and the law

(Self-counsel legal series)
ISBN 0-88908-785-7

    1. Law and art. 2. Artists — Legal status, laws, etc. —
Canada. 3. Art — Collectors and collecting — Canada.
I. Smart, Stephen B. (Stephen Beverley), 1944-
II. Baxter, Mary, 1962- III. Title. IV. Series.
KE3968.A77 1994   344.71'097   C94-910286-5
KF4288.A77 1994

Self-Counsel Press
(*a division of*)·
International Self-Counsel Press Ltd.

Head and Editorial Office	U.S. Address
1481 Charlotte Road	1704 N. State Street
North Vancouver, B.C. V7J 1H1	Bellingham, WA 98225

CONTENTS

NOTICE TO READERS

Laws are constantly changing. Every effort is made to keep this publication as current as possible. However, neither the author nor the publisher can accept any responsibility for changes to the law or practice that occur after the printing of this publication. Please be sure that you have the most recent edition.

INTRODUCTION

When we began research for this book, we were already aware of a number of good publications available that examined certain aspects of the art market in Canada and that provided practical advice to those interested in making, selling, collecting, and exhibiting art. But the majority of these publications addressed only the interests of a singular specialized audience such as artists, collectors, or museum professionals. Very little has been written on the market itself, or how the market's participants interact — what obligations are involved or how certain activities affect other ones.

Knowledge of the roles of the different participants in the art market and how they interact is crucial to all of those involved, as well as to those interested in becoming involved. Knowing how a collector goes about acquiring work and what concerns may feature in their selection of art may help artists and dealers in their development of marketing strategies. Collectors may gain a greater appreciation of the works they acquire when they take into account the factors that influence artistic production.

Being aware of the different ways in which our courts view art is an important prerequisite for all those interested in creating, marketing, acquiring, and disposing of art. Moreover, we have found that all of those involved regularly take on more than one role. For example, artists frequently act as sales agents to market their work and they, along with art dealers, often collect other artists' work.

For these reasons, we decided to structure this book around the life of a work of art. It follows issues that touch on works of art from creation through their life until they are either re-sold or donated. This unique approach enabled us to outline the business and legal obligations that affect those who create, own, market, or donate art.

This book is intended for anyone with an interest in the visual arts, whether that interest involves an occasional trip to the art gallery or a more professional commitment. For the artist, this book offers practical advice on the day-to-day business of making art, including selecting a space that works best for you, how to hire an assistant, what to look for in a sales agent, and what goes into negotiating business agreements. We have also provided discussions of relevant issues such as copyright and obscenity legislation.

This book also contains practical advice about acquiring and maintaining a collection for both the beginning and experienced collector. We suggest where to look for good advice, how to go about planning a collection, and what to consider when insuring, donating, or commissioning artwork. We also discuss how tax issues, estate planning, and family matters such as marriage and divorce might affect your art collection.

Anyone in the commercial end of the market can find information on how their peers create and maintain good working relationships with both artists and clients. Those involved in public institutions or wishing to develop public venues will find discussions on strategies for acquiring art and how to create a venue that best suits the interests of your community.

There are other issues that we may not have touched on, but it would be impossible to describe how everyone does business. Success in the art market relies on intuition and entrepreneurial flair rather than conformation to a standardized system. What we can offer, however, is a general introduction to the art market and solid advice from seasoned professionals who have made the visual arts their business as well as their passion.

Stephen B. Smart and Mary Baxter

1

THE BUSINESS OF CREATING ART

by Mary Baxter

Creating art is a wonderful, mysterious process. There is little known about how an artist is inspired to choose one material over another to create a work or how the decision is made to combine certain shapes or ideas. We may never know how these imaginative leaps are made.

But making art is also a business — big business in places like New York and London — and questions regarding the business of creating art can, for the most part, be answered. These include issues such as which business structure is best, arranging studio space, how to market an artist's work, working with an assistant, insurance concerns, and so on.

Often it is hard for the artist to come to terms with the business aspect of making art. While universities and colleges now include some marketing courses in their fine arts curriculums, many of those who graduate still operate under the impression that making art involves a certain way of living. We have all heard of the starving artist living in a lonely garret and of the long-term suppression of artists who do not toe the party line in places like the former Soviet Union. We tend to accept their role in society as spiritual rather than economic; they are visionaries rather than practitioners.

However, most artists do not really live in garrets, and many artists rely on the help of assistants to create and fabricate their work. For all the ideals they might espouse, they still have to pay rent, eat, and make enough money to buy their materials. Stripped of the romance, making art is, in effect, a small business: a product is being created for public consumption.

Of course there is much more involved in the making of art than realizing a profit. In fact, very few artists will ever make a profit on their work. But adopting a businesslike approach to making art has important psychological and practical benefits. Treating your work as a business helps you develop a professional attitude, which permits you to maintain a practical, organized approach to the marketing of your work. It helps you set goals and evaluate your needs in a practical manner. There is nothing wrong with treating yourself as an entrepreneur: many of the most noted artists in the history of art were also successful businessmen — take Rembrandt or Michelangelo, for example.

These issues are discussed generally in this chapter, as they affect all artists. Where more specific information is required, you might want to refer to some of the many guides now available that offer solid, thoughtful advice. Where appropriate, these guides are referred to in the discussion below. In some cases, of course, professional advice may be needed.

a. TAKING CARE OF BUSINESS

Filing annual income tax returns. Making quarterly installments. Balancing accounts and keeping track of inventory. These aren't usually at the top of an artist's "fun things to do" list. Often these tasks are left to the last moment and are rushed through, which can lead to errors that sometimes involve weeks of administrative headaches. Rushing also means that the artist does not have the time to figure out how to take advantage of tax breaks that may be available.

Spending a little time once every couple of weeks can help prevent mix-ups and, in the end, save a considerable amount of time. It can also give the artist the peace of mind to get on with the business of creating. The sections below discuss some of the main areas of concern for artists and their businesses.

1. Do you need to incorporate?

Artists generally have little need to incorporate their businesses, and very few do. Incorporation means creating a business that has its own, autonomous legal identity. In the eyes of the law, the business is subject to many of the same rights, privileges, and obligations that apply to an individual. For example, like the individual, an incorporated business must pay taxes.

There are a number of reasons why an artist might consider incorporation:

(a) For artists who achieve considerable financial success and have very high incomes, incorporation may assist with tax planning. (For a business that is not incorporated, earnings are taxed at the personal tax rate.)

(b) Incorporating a business helps insulate its owners from personal liability. For example, if the business goes bankrupt, the owners are not obliged to pay the debts out of their personal savings; their liability for the debts of the business is generally limited to the amount they have already invested in it. Similarly, owners of a business are generally not liable beyond their existing investment for accidents occurring in the course of business. Artists who use unconventional materials such as toxic or radioactive substances, or who create works that might expose the public to risk, might consider incorporating to limit potential liability to the corporate entity as opposed to exposing themselves personally. Personal liability can still arise, however, to the extent the artist participates directly in the act that gave rise to the liability, and directors of a corporation are, under law, still responsible for certain liabilities.

3

(c) Incorporation can be beneficial to artists working in collectives because it ensures that responsibilities are evenly divided and that no one individual assumes too great a financial burden. Moreover, if the collective is involved in exhibiting or sponsoring artwork or programming an exhibition space, incorporation may lend the collective a certain validity in the eyes of the potential sponsors.

Instead of incorporation, an artist may choose to work as a sole proprietor and simply apply for any necessary licences to do business. For example, artists interested in operating a retail outlet, such as a commercial gallery, must apply for a retail licence from the appropriate municipal authorities.

Unincorporated businesses should also register their business name with the appropriate government authorities. However, registration does not give the artist any right in the name. An artist should consider registering a business name as a trademark, which would prevent others using it, if the name is particularly important or valuable.

Artists interested in what benefits incorporation might offer should discuss the matter with a lawyer or an accountant. You may also want to refer to the *Incorporation Guide* for your province which are published by Self-Counsel Press.

2. Keeping records

Like any other business person, artists should keep records for two basic reasons. First, records are needed to compile figures for tax purposes and to keep track of income. Second, records are needed to keep track of inventory.

(a) Records for tax purposes

The Income Tax Act provides a number of tax breaks for artists, but without the proper records in place, it is impossible to calculate or substantiate a claim, let alone take advantage of the breaks offered. Moreover, without maintaining some sort of recording system, the artist might lose track of money owed him or her.

Keeping track of income and expenses usually involves two kinds of records: a written account of income and expenses, and a file of actual receipts and invoices to document the written account. At year-end, these two records are compared to ensure each is accurate.

Of the two records, the file of receipts and invoices is more important because documents are needed to substantiate claims if you, the artist, are audited by the tax department. If you wish to claim an expense against income, for example, you must be able to prove that the expense was incurred, which is usually done by providing the verifying documents. Keeping the two records, however, provides a safety net in case original documents are lost.

The written account does not have to be complicated: it can even consist of the entries in your cheque book. An accordion file purchased from a local stationery store is all that is needed to file the documents substantiating the written account. If you do your filing daily, the work will be minimal and the year-end process of compiling records for tax purposes will be simple.

You should keep these documents on file:

(a) Copies of all invoices and receipts for sales made

(b) Copies of all expense receipts regarding the day-to-day operation of the business

(c) A record of GST paid on purchases and charged on sales (if you are registered for the GST — see chapter 11)

(d) An ongoing record of any money owed to you.

If your work is in the hands of a dealer, it is wise to request regular updates regarding any individuals or businesses that have purchased your work.

(b) Inventory records

Keep track of your inventory because knowing what you have and where it's located means business transactions can be conducted with a minimum of fuss. As well, inventory documentation is also required by insurance companies. It pays to design a system of inventory control and to follow through on it to avoid potential problems.

The inventory record should include a physical description of each work, its value, and its current location. If work is consigned to an art dealer, you, as the artist, should insist on receiving written quarterly inventory reports so you are always aware of where your inventory is.

b. THE BUSINESS OF FINDING A WORK SPACE

Before an artist can turn to the challenge of finding the right venue for marketing his or her work, which is probably the foremost consideration for most artists, he or she must first find an appropriate place to work. Having to consider cost, space, privacy, zoning requirements, and even safety issues can make the search for suitable accommodation problematic.

1. What's available? What's appropriate?

Due to financial constraints, a lot of artists make do by turning a portion of their living space into a studio. Others augment their home studios with stints at professional facilities such as print or video workshops or metal foundries. Space is at a premium in countries such as Britain and Ireland; many artists there rely on the facilities their arts councils provide, or they count on month-long stays at retreats such as the Tyrone Guthrie Centre in rural Ireland for the peace and quiet to develop their ideas.

In North America, many artists at the beginning of their careers house themselves in graduate schools, which are valued as much for the opportunities they provide to work undisturbed alongside other artists as they are for their educational functions. Achieving a Masters in Fine Arts is also the way many artists qualify themselves for teaching positions at colleges or universities — by far the job of choice for supporting artistic activities. Teaching in such institutions can often provide the continued use of good facilities and, space permitting, a studio free of charge.

There are many alternatives to the studio loft or warehouse space that artists seem almost obligated to obtain. Developing the right kind of space to suit the artist's needs boils down to evaluating what is needed and considering the ways these needs can be met. An artist who produces drawings, for example, may not need the elaborate and expensive setup of a private studio. A sculptor who relies on independent contractors may need a large space on a temporary basis to assemble or store work, but may be able to set aside space within the home for working on the development of ideas. In these cases, maintaining an off-residence studio would be expensive in relation to the benefits it would provide. It may be better for the artist to find a living situation that allows enough privacy to work out ideas and enough space to accommodate a limited amount of "messing about."

Making these decisions, however, depends on the kind of art you make and the kind of person you are. Separating the place of work from the place of residence is important to many people. Those with families find it extremely difficult to achieve the privacy needed to do their own work. Others find that with the studio so close at hand they do nothing but work. Still others find that a physical division between work and residence helps motivate them.

2. Zoning requirements

Whether you live deep in the interior of British Columbia or in the heart of downtown Ottawa, your local municipality controls the way in which you can use the land. The municipality classifies land by use: commercial, residential, or industrial, for example. How the land is classified determines what kind of taxes owners pay to the municipality, what kind of buildings can be developed (the number, size, and projected use), and what occupancy standards apply to the buildings regarding safety, etc.

For example, it is illegal to live in a building in a commercial zone because the safety standards that apply are not as comprehensive as those for residential property. Similarly, operating a retail outlet from a residential property without first checking whether or not an application for rezoning is needed can pose legal problems because taxes for commercial and residential properties are structured differently.

It is, therefore, extremely important to determine the zoning regulations that apply to the property on which you locate your studio. Those preferring to work in their homes must establish what kinds of activities are permitted.

For those artists planning to build their own studio, or to renovate an existing structure to suit their needs, a building permit, which is obtained from the building inspection department of the municipality, is usually required. Altering the use of an existing structure or adding another building to a property can pose problems.

Those who are interested in renting space for a studio will most likely be searching for space in a building with commercial, mixed-use commercial, or industrial zoning. In all provinces, anyone who leases commercial property must rely on a lease agreement to establish their rights and the landlord's obligations.

A commercial lease is quite different from a residential lease. Most provinces provide protection of the residential tenant's rights, and the laws that establish these rights can take precedence over a rental agreement if the terms of that agreement are contrary to the applicable laws. Not so when the property is commercial. Parties to a lease for commercial property are bound by its terms. The importance of working out all aspects of the agreement with the landlord and putting the agreement in writing cannot be stressed enough. If the agreement is not recorded, the tenant has no protection.

The following are some of questions that might arise during the negotiation of a lease:

(a) *Does the landlord have to know what I'm going to use the space for?*

Yes. If your activities may affect the space in any way, you must first obtain permission from the landlord. Renovation of the space must be cleared with the landlord. These details and the landlord's permission must be noted in the lease agreement. You might also wish to obtain the landlord's assurance that your intended use will not contravene any zoning legislation.

(b) *Can I live there?*

If you obtain the landlord's permission, and it is recorded in the lease, yes. Most landlords, however, will not allow you to live there because it is in conflict with the zoning bylaws and they could be fined. Moreover, even if a municipality agrees to a change in zoning, owners of commercial property are usually unwilling to accommodate a residential tenant because they would probably have to comply with more rigorous (and expensive) safety standards. If you choose to live in the space without obtaining the landlord's written permission, you are violating the leasing agreement and the landlord has the right to evict you.

(c) *Besides rent, what bills am I responsible for when I sign a lease?*

You may find yourself responsible for paying all or portions of the utilities, repairs to premises, operating costs of premises, municipal realty taxes, and insurance. Keep in mind that the lease for commercial property can and should be negotiated. For example, you might agree to pay a portion of the taxes or help maintain the building in exchange for a lower rent.

(d) *What is the landlord responsible for?*

The landlord is responsible for whatever items are negotiated in the lease. Do not be afraid to negotiate.

Always have your lease agreement checked by a lawyer before signing. Always ensure that a written lease agreement is in place if you are renting non-residential property.

Useful additional information about housing issues for artists is supplied in the book, *The Artists' Studio and Housing Handbook,* by Dino Tsantis (Toronto: Canadian Artists Representation for Ontario (CARO), 1985).

c. MARKETING YOUR ART

The concept of marketing art is often foreign to artists. Many contemporary artists find it difficult to put a price tag on their work because the motivation for making art is often not driven by commercial demands. In fact, current thinking regards the artist as society's visionary — the gifted individual who offers new perspectives on many of the things we take for granted. This social function cannot really be translated into economic terms.

Moreover, for the majority of fine artists, making art does not make money, plain and simple. Anyone involved in the visual arts rarely measures an artist's success in financial terms. More often than not it is reputation and critical acclaim that counts. Critical recognition, however, in turn leads to more people being interested in acquiring an artist's work, and increased demand usually translates into higher sale prices. Therefore, even though those making and looking at art may not be motivated by dollars and cents, their activities and ambitions may eventually result in financialcompensation.

1. Getting exposure

The most important thing to keep in mind when trying to establish your reputation or market your work is that *if you don't show your work, no one will see it.* This may seem obvious, but it is surprising the number of artists who wait for opportunity to knock on their door, and then become bitter when it doesn't. Taking advantage of opportunities as they arise and demonstrating initiative in promoting artwork are steps every artist must take, regardless of whether their interests are in achieving critical or financial success.

For many, the first opportunity to exhibit their work occurs in the facility where they receive training. Your art teacher is not only your first important mentor, but also the first person connected to the art world who can spread word of your talent. A number of well-known artists at work today received their first recognition while studying at university or college.

The graduate exhibition that is usually required to complete a Masters of Fine Arts can also be an important moment in the fledgling artist's career. The artist can reveal a body of work and demonstrate the range of his or her artistic approach. For most artists, it may be years before another opportunity for a solo exhibition arises.

In the "real world," finding opportunities to exhibit work can be difficult. Sending work to juried exhibitions is one way to gain exposure. A juried exhibition is essentially a contest in which one or more arts professionals (usually curators or artists) choose a few works of art from a number of submissions. These exhibitions may be limited to a particular medium or based on a certain theme — artists located in a particular region, for example. They may be run by public institutions such as art galleries, or professional associations such as the Ontario Society of Artists.

It is harder to get work into group exhibitions because they are usually organized by a curator who has a specific theme and particular artists in mind. Occasionally, the curator may issue a call for artists whose work deals with the show's theme, but usually the curator will rely on his or her research into the arts community to determine who to include.

The first step, therefore, is to tap into the facilities, institutions, and publications that post listings for these opportunities. Local public art galleries, universities and colleges that have visual arts programs, and trade magazines are all good sources. As well, arts organizations such as Visual Arts Ontario and the Canadian Crafts Council regularly inform their members of exhibition or commissioning opportunities through their publications.

Many artists also find it helpful to work or volunteer with an arts organization at the beginning of their careers. This is a way to earn income, learn about other facets of the visual arts, and build up contacts with those in the arts community. It also provides the artist with an opportunity to observe how the exhibition process works and to see which approaches to promoting artwork are more successful than others.

Many of the artists who have emerged on the forefront of the Canadian arts scene have relied on their ingenuity to find ways to present their work to the public. Artist's studios, laundromats, parking garages, old department stores, and restaurants have all been used as venues for exhibiting the work of emerging artists in recent years. Depending on their policy, public libraries, which often maintain a small exhibition space, will sometimes lend their space to an artist free of charge. Exhibiting work in a space that bears some sort of relationship to the artist's subject matter — like an artist who uses children as a subject exhibiting pieces in a day care facility, for example — is another angle to consider. These kinds of spaces provide artists with a means of reaching an audience that may not be inclined to visit more traditional art venues.

As the artist, you must organize and fund this type of exhibition, so think about what you ultimately want out of it. Are you trying to reach a particular audience? Are you trying to sell your work? Is the exhibition an artistic statement?

Setting clear goals for your exhibition will help in the promotion of the exhibition. Figuring out what your motivations might be — whether you are interested in reaching an audience not usually involved in the visual arts, achieving critical recognition, or selling your artwork — helps you target sources of publicity and formulate a publicity strategy.

The publicity tools normally used in the promotion of an exhibition might include any or all of the following:

(a) An invitation that includes the details of the exhibition (when, where, by whom, contact number, etc.) and a reproduction of an image from one of the works in the show

(b) A press release describing the theme of the exhibition as well as all of the information contained in the invitation

(c) A pictorial or video catalogue of the work exhibited and an analysis of the artist's work

(d) An opening or one-time event to which members of the targeted audience, prospective collectors, and members of the press and/or art critics are specifically invited to meet with the artist

(e) A listing of media and arts professionals to which the media package should be sent

(f) An invitation list (which should include media and arts professionals to remind them of the exhibition)

(g) Paid advertisements in media that is popular with your target audience

Organizing your publicity strategy is relatively easy; organizing your publicity strategy to have an impact is difficult.

The media, no matter how genuine their interest, have many demands and competing interests on their time. Although your publicity package may make them interested in your work, another source, such as a respected arts professional, can make all the difference in motivating a critic to attend your opening. For better or worse, word of mouth is an important, if not crucial, factor in achieving critical success for your exhibition.

A word of caution: hounding art critics may have the opposite effect from the one you are hoping to achieve. Get other people to hound them, people whose independent opinions the critics will respect.

Timing is another important factor. People may forget about an exhibition if invitations are sent out too early, but if notified too close to the event, they may not be able to work the exhibition into their schedules. Build up publicity by organizing advertisements or notices to appear one month, two weeks, one week in advance, and during the week of the event. Sending out invitations and media packages two weeks before the event is generally the most successful strategy.

Finally, don't be disappointed if the big wigs don't show up. Think about those who came, responded to your work, and might give you positive recommendations in the future. Building a reputation and/or selling artwork does not happen overnight!

2. Artist collectives

Many artists band together with other artists to share the responsibilities of organizing an exhibition. Some of these groups have had an enormous impact on the art scene in Canada. Many groups have gone on to form artist-run centres that regularly mount exhibitions of their work and the work of other artists. A Space in Toronto, Eye Level Gallery in Halifax, and Western Front in Vancouver are three such venues that began this way and continue to be pace-setters in the contemporary Canadian art scene.

By banding together, artists share the responsibilities of promoting their work and increase their opportunities. They can share their contacts with each other and broaden their audience base.. Most important, they can provide for each other a nurturing network of support. For more information on artist-run centres, contact —

Association of National Non-Profit Run Centres
(ANNPAC/RACA)
183 Bathurst Street
Main Floor
Toronto, Ontario
M5T 2R7

Finally, most artist-run centres have a programmed exhibition space. They are supportive of the work of emerging artists (provided the work meets the mandate of their centre), and often provide new artists with their first exhibition. In searching for a venue, these centres are among the first places to contact.

3. Public art projects

Another way to put your work into the public eye is to devise a public art project. You must first gain permission from the public agency that controls the area where you want to locate the project. Most public agencies are enthusiastic about public art projects, as long as they don't have to foot the bill and you comply with their requirements.

From time to time, some municipal governments, such as the cities of Toronto, Halifax, Calgary, and Vancouver, release funds for temporary and permanent public art projects. The best way to find out if your municipality has a public art program is to ask.

4. Selling your own work

While many artists rely on an agent or dealer to sell their work, others have managed to sell their own. Those that are most successful tend to focus on a particular skill (portraiture, for example) or a particular subject (wildlife or scenic depictions of a particular area.)

Many of these artists set up their own galleries, conduct sales, or arrange commissions themselves. Often they develop a loyal following of collectors who advertise their work through word of mouth and/or buy art on an ongoing basis.

Artists who represent themselves undertake two demanding jobs: producing and selling art. It is, therefore, extremely important to manage time carefully. For instance, artists who depict a particular area often live in that area and sell their work to visitors. In the off season, they produce their artwork and during the tourist season they concentrate on selling their work.

For those working on a commission basis, such as portrait artists, it is harder to keep the two functions separate. Each client may yield future clients and the artist must be available for any potential business.

5. Art dealers

For many artists, finding an art dealer is the ideal way to sell their art. Getting a commercial dealer to represent your work, however, may be difficult.

Although it is the rare dealer who does not have a great passion for visual art, an art dealer is first and foremost a business person, interested in making a living, if not a profit. Each time a dealer takes on a new artist, it is a risk. Dealers look for certain markers to indicate that the artist will reap sound financial rewards for them.

Generally, art dealers look for a commitment to making art, which is usually demonstrated in the artist having built up a large body of work. In the eyes of the dealer, an artist who has sought out opportunities, sought education, and achieved some critical recognition is a much better bet than one who hasn't done any of the above. For further discussion of the artist/dealer relationship, see chapter 4.

6. Price structures

Deciding on a price for artwork involves a number of factors including production costs of material and labor, experience, exhibition record, market demand, and dealer commissions.

Gauging how these factors interrelate is the key to evolving a solid pricing structure for your work. Someone who gave up ten years of life to create one sculpture, for instance, cannot hope to recoup the cost of labor because it would be far beyond what even the richest of collectors might consider paying. A painter who spends five minutes creating a watercolor likewise would not want to base the price on the cost of materials and labor. In this case, the length of time it took to produce the work does not necessarily reflect the quality or the number of years the artist spent honing his or her craft.

The best way to gauge what the market is willing to pay is to check the prices of similar work by artists who are at approximately the same stage of their careers and who sell to a similar clientele. Be careful to allow for the cost of framing when surveying prices.

When and how much to raise prices are other issues artists often encounter. Generally, prices are raised when the artist receives critical recognition. A major exhibition at a prominent public art gallery, or the winning of a prestigious award, for example, often provide a reason to raise prices because these distinctions will result in a greater demand for the artist's work. In fact, any time there is an escalation in demand, the artist might consider raising prices, provided there are solid reasons to expect the demand to continue.

Artists who are just entering the market must also be careful to allow for growth in their prices. An unknown artist who sets too high a price for his or her work may discourage collectors who, for a slightly lower price, may have been willing to make a purchase. Also, if you discover that your work isn't selling because the price is too high, it is extremely difficult, if not impossible, to lower your prices for future work.

Keeping prices consistent is also important. It is extremely bad business practice to sell essentially the same item to a number of people for different amounts.

7. Developing your promotional package

As an artist, you will need to present some sort of package that introduces your work and experience. Many art professionals and collectors use these packages to supplement their research or provide information about acquisitions. Such a package typically includes the following:

(a) Complete resume (including exhibitions, commissions, collections in which your work is included, reviews, etc.)

(b) Ten to fifteen slides of your work appropriately labeled

(c) Copies of any published analysis of your work

(d) A concise statement describing your artistic approach

In addition, some artists include a video catalogue of their works.

Before sending out your package, it is extremely important to research the individual or institution you are sending it to. Does your work fit their exhibition or collection guidelines? What other information might they require? *Never send out original material, unless specifically requested.* Even when you are requested to send original artwork or documents, you should always make sure you understand why originals have been requested (a juried exhibition, for instance, is usually chosen from original artwork), and arrange in advance how they will be returned, who is responsible for their return, and, in the case of original artwork, whose insurance policy covers it while it is out of the artist's studio.

8. Public museum collections

There are many public museums that acquire art to add to their collections. Selection is based on art that meets the criteria of the collection mandate. If the collection is based on regional artists, for instance, the work of regional artists will be purchased. But if the collection is based on a particular medium, the museum will purchase works done in that medium with no attention paid to the geographical location of the artist.

Art considered for purchase is usually presented by the gallery's curator to be reviewed by the gallery's acquisition committee. This committee usually consists of gallery members who have knowledge of the art market or some sort of experience with the visual arts.

For many artists, being included in a specific museum collection can do much to promote their reputation. Public museums, however, do not generally purchase a great amount of art because their funds are limited. Also, because they are public institutions, museums must be careful in how they add to their collections. A considerable amount of time, research, and deliberation goes into their decisions to purchase. If a museum cannot spare the funds to acquire an artist's work, and the artist would like to see the work in the museum's collection, donation should be considered. (See chapter 9 for a discussion on the benefits of donating art.)

9. Corporate collectors

Because of the tremendous growth in corporate collecting during the seventies and eighties, corporations are often regarded as "the last of the big-time spenders" by artists. Any artist — especially one beginning a career — who has tried selling directly to a corporation, however, will tell a different story.

Corporations are generally conservative in their tastes. They prefer to purchase the work of artists with a proven track record and usually conduct business with established art dealers. Moreover, a corporate art collection is often restricted by the size of its business premises; art collection often ends for corporations when the space allotted has been filled up. As a result, many corporations are now shifting from collecting art to sponsoring exhibitions as a way to support the visual arts.

10. Art banks and public gallery rental programs

The Canada Council Art Bank regularly purchases art and rents it to government organizations and non-profit institutions. Art that is submitted for consideration is selected by a jury of artists. For further information, write to —

The Canada Council Art Bank
370 Catherine Street
P.O. Box 1047
Ottawa, Ontario
K1P 5V8

Some municipal and provincial governments operate their own art banks as well. These banks generally limit their selection to artists living within their jurisdiction.

Many public art galleries operate art rental programs, which provide another marketing opportunity for artists. The gallery does not purchase artwork, but negotiates the rental and/or sale of works for the artist. Many artists have had success in selling and renting their work through art rental programs.

Selection procedures for art rental programs vary from gallery to gallery. If you are interested in participating in an art rental program, contact the particular gallery for details.

d. ARTISTS AND ASSISTANTS

A 1993 issue of *Art in America* brought to light just how many contemporary artists rely on the help of others to create their work. In the past it was commonly understood that artists employed studio assistants and apprentices to help them with anything from preparing canvases and grinding pigment to painting portions of a commission. But in more modern times we tend to assume that artists work long, lonely hours in the studio using their own hands to create art from scratch.

Many artists do work alone. However, just as many, if not more, employ assistants or use specialized manufacturers to build some of the components of their work.

Often artists are reluctant to talk about their use of outside assistance because they fear it might somehow affect the value of their work. But given the highly complex, labor-intensive methods often used to create art, outside assistance may be a necessity, not a luxury. Some artists, such as painters or print makers, need short-term assistance to help prepare canvases or pull prints. Artists who combine different media, or who are involved in public commissions, inevitably require assistance in the construction and installation of their work. Canadian artist Micah Lexier, for example, in the video production *Public Art at Metrocentre,* compares the way he works to an architect "who designs [a work], figures it out, acts as the contractor and other people fabricate it."

1. Where to find help — and giving proper credit

Many artists hire students or recent graduates who use the opportunity to gain experience, knowledge, and contacts. Friends, or friends of friends, who are professional artists in their own right are often contacted to help out with special tasks, such as the installation of an exhibition or the assembling of a sculpture in its permanent setting.

Wade Saunders, an American artist and critic, recommends (in *Art in America* February, 1993) hiring people who have specialized skills, rather than professional artists. While he agrees that a professionally trained artist will be sensitive to the needs of the employer, he also makes the point that artists usually stay as long as it takes to launch their own career. People who have specialized skills, on the other hand, bring to the job the required expertise and a different kind of ambition.

Moreover, if the employment relationship is good, assistants will often remain for years. Such long-term assistants become invaluable. Anne Poirier, a prominent French artist has commented that assistants become "a part of the work."

But for many artists who use assistants, there arises the question of how to give them proper credit. Micah Lexier solves this problem by not signing his work because he feels it is made by someone else. Other artists, such as Brian Scott, a Toronto photographer, ensure that the name of the assistant appears on any credits accompanying the work.

2. The artist as an employer

In order to avoid paying benefits, most artists arrange to subcontract labor rather than hire employees. Yet beyond providing an escape from taxation, most artists do not really understand the legal differences between subcontracting and hiring, and that can lead to problems.

When you, the artist, subcontract work, you contract for the services of an independent contractor, rather than enter into a contract with an employee. You are engaging a service, not an individual. In this way you avoid many of the obligations that you would have if you were hiring an employee, such as providing a minimum wage, vacation pay, regular hours of work, etc. Nor are you responsible for making unemployment insurance or Canada Pension Plan contributions on behalf of the individual.

No matter which route you decide to take, the terms of the relationship must be made clear. Even if you are engaging someone to work only on an occasional basis, you may be required to comply with the requirements of your provincial employment standards legislation.

In Ontario, for example, employees working for artists may be regarded as full-time, part-time, temporary, or homeworkers. (Homeworkers are people who work in their own homes creating, assembling, repairing, etc. articles or materials.) If they are employees who fall into any of these categories, their rights are protected by the Ontario Employment Standards Act, which controls employment issues such as maximum hours of work in a day or week, overtime pay, minimum wages, public holidays, vacations with pay, equal pay for male and female employees, employee benefit plans, pregnancy and parental leave, notice of termination of employment, and severance pay.

3. Put it in writing

A relationship between an artist and worker can be established in writing or conversation. For your own protection, record the details of your agreement.

Any agreement should, of course, make reference to the type of work the individual is to perform and the method of payment. Here are some other details which should be discussed and clarified:

(a) Are you engaging the individual as an independent contractor or employee?

(b) Will the individual be using special equipment or hazardous materials? If so, does he or she have proper training?

(c) Does the individual have workers' compensation coverage?

4. Ensuring the safety of your assistants

Whether you hire an independent contractor or an employee, you are responsible for the welfare of that individual in your workplace. A workplace is where the independent contractor or employee performs his or her services. If you have asked the person to help you assemble a sculpture on a waterfront, this becomes the workplace. If, however, the individual works at his or her own premises, then it is the individual, not you, who is responsible for ensuring safety and welfare on the job.

Responsibility of the employer or contractor regarding the welfare of the worker is controlled by provincial occupational health and safety legislation, and artists should refer to the appropriate legislation for specifics. Generally, artists should expect to —

(a) inform workers about potential hazards,

(b) train and supervise workers to protect their health and safety,

(c) take every reasonable precaution in the circumstances for the protection of a worker,

(d) ensure that the physical structure of the workplace can support all loads to which it may be subjected,

(e) provide and maintain in good condition any equipment and materials, and

(f) comply with a prescribed standard that limits the exposure of a worker to biological, chemical, or physical agents.

The last item is a specific concern to a number of artists. Artists must be extremely careful to consider the kinds of materials or equipment they are using. Hazardous materials and heavy equipment may require special surroundings such as additional ventilation or reinforced flooring. It is false economy to avoid outfitting the workplace with proper safety features; and it is plain stupidity to expose yourself or others to potentially hazardous materials or dangerous situations. In these cases it is crucial for the artist to make a definite, physical division between home and the workplace.

The Workplace Hazardous Materials Information System (WHMIS) is a provincial and federally regulated system used to disseminate information regarding hazardous materials to employers and workers. Through a combination of federal and provincial acts, it ensures that hazardous materials (e.g., compressed gas, or flammable, combustible, oxidizing, poisonous, infectious, corrosive, or dangerously reactive materials) are properly labelled and safely handled within the workplace.

Failure to comply with the standards of WHMIS can lead to a warning. If the warning is not heeded, the controlled product may be seized and, on occasion, prosecution may result. In Ontario, WHMIS is usually enforced by inspectors with the provincial Ministry of Labour. Obtain a guide to the WHMIS which, in Ontario, is made available through the Ministry of Labour.

Restrictions regarding safe conduct within the workplace are there for a reason. For example, it is well-known that the health problems experienced by many print makers can be attributed to handling printing materials without observing the proper safety precautions. Other traditional materials, such as oil paints, can cause severe problems if not handled properly. More now than ever, artists are exploring new materials and technologies to aid in the creation of art. No work of art, however, is worth the destruction of an individual's long-term health.

5. Insurance

As the artist, you may also be responsible for registering for workers' compensation coverage if you employ workers. The Workers' Compensation Board is a provincially run no-fault insurance system which provides benefits to workers who are injured on the job. As an artist employing others, this insurance is extremely important to consider. Failure to arrange coverage could put you, the employer, at great risk because you would be liable for any injuries occurring in your workplace.

Provincial workers' compensation legislation places an obligation on the principle contractor to ensure that contract workers are registered under the act. Therefore, if you are subcontracting work undertaken in your workplace, you must ensure that those workers are properly covered. This does not necessarily mean that you have to include them under your workers' compensation coverage, but you may need to ensure that the independent contractor has arranged his or her own insurance coverage.

Employers who contribute to the workers' compensation fund cannot be sued by a worker who receives an injury on the job. Personal insurance that covers the workplace can also be considered as an alternative or complement to workers' compensation coverage.

It is also in the artist's best interest to purchase some form of insurance that covers artwork, studio equipment, and the studio if it is owned by the artist. Art and studio equipment can get damaged or stolen and can be expensive to repair or replace.

In Ontario, Visual Arts Ontario offers the artist a personal insurance package as well as an art and transport package. For more information regarding these packages, contact —

Visual Arts Ontario
439 Wellington Street W.
Third Floor
Toronto, Ontario
M5V 1E7

There are many other insurance packages available. A licensed insurance broker should be consulted to help you decide which might best suit your needs.

For more general information about the business concerns of artists, you may want to refer to the book, *Information for Artists: A Practical Guide for Visual Artists,* edited by Sarah Yates (Toronto: Canadian Artists Representation for Ontario, 1989). CARO has also produced many other useful publications on business and legal issues affecting artists. For information, write to —

Canadian Artists Representation for Ontario (CARO)
183 Bathurst Street
Toronto, Ontario
M5T 2R4

2

COPYRIGHT LAW

by Glen A. Bloom

Simply put, copyright is a "bundle" of legal rights given to creators to reproduce their artwork. These rights exist and are protected under the federal Copyright Act. The act also establishes a regime for the protection of certain *moral rights* of creators, which are rights personal to the creator different in nature from copyright.

However, the mere fact that an artist creates an artwork or a performance that has artistic and aesthetic merit does not, by itself, convey copyright protection. To determine whether copyright exists, the artist must refer to applicable sections of the Copyright Act.

Canada's Copyright Act came into force in 1924 and it has been substantially amended only one time since then, in 1988. The 1988 amendment was intended as the first of two phases of copyright revision. The second phase, likely to contain controversial provisions in modernizing Canada's laws, may not be introduced into Parliament or enacted for a number of years.

As a result, Canada's copyright law, the foundation of artists' rights, is seriously out of date. While it addresses many of the fields of modern artistic endeavor (e.g., paintings, drawings, sculptures, works of artistic craftsmanship, and photographs), it also speaks in archaic terms: protection for "perforated roles," "contrivances by means of which the work may be mechanically performed or delivered," "cinematographic production," and "contrivances by means of which sounds may be mechanically reproduced." It does *not* speak of videotapes or compact discs, and it clearly fails to take into account the multi-faceted nature of contemporary artistic endeavor.

Fortunately for artists and creators, our courts have been able to extend and apply copyright to some contemporary creative endeavors, such as computer software. But the courts are restricted by the language of the Copyright Act and, therefore, their means of extending protection to emerging technologies and artistic endeavors are limited. Artists and owners of works continue to be left uncertain about the copyright protection of their works.

When considering copyright, two points should be kept in mind. First, the Copyright Act governs works in the artistic domain and works of commercial application such as computer software. In other words, copyright is not a question of whether the work is regarded by the artist or the artistic community as having artistic or aesthetic merit. Second, Canada's copyright laws seek to create a balance between the rights of creators and the interest of the public to access copyright works and to use copyright.

In this chapter, the terms "author," "artist," and "creator" are used interchangeably to mean the individual who creates a work to which copyright may attach.

a. UNDERSTANDING THE GENERAL PRINCIPLES OF COPYRIGHT LAW

1. How copyright arises

Copyright applies only to original literary, dramatic, musical, and artistic works and, to a lesser extent, to devices that reproduce sound (referred to in the legislation as "contrivances by means of which sounds may be mechanically reproduced" and which include, for example, videotape, to the extent that it may be used to reproduce sound.) The work must be original, which does *not* mean that the work did not previously exist. Instead, all that is required is that the work be created by the author without merely copying from the work of another. For example, if two artists created identical paintings, but without one copying from the other, each artist would be entitled to claim copyright in his or her respective painting. It is not necessary to formally register or give notice of a claim of copyright; copyright exists the moment an artist's work comes into being.

There are two conditions that must be met for copyright to apply in Canada. First, the author must be one or more of the following —

(a)   a Canadian citizen or other British subject,

(b)   a citizen or subject of one of the countries that adheres to the Berne Convention, an international copyright convention, or

(c)   a citizen or subject of a country to which the Canadian government has extended the benefit of Canadian copyright, or a resident within "Her Majesty's realms and territories," (in effect, the Commonwealth).

For example, an artist who is a Canadian citizen acquires copyright in Canada for a painting that he or she created anywhere in the world. An artist who is a French citizen acquires copyright in Canada for a painting that the artist created in France or anywhere else in the world. But an artist who is a citizen of Bahrain who creates a painting in Bahrain does *not* acquire copyright in Canada because Bahrain is not a member of the Berne Convention and Canada has not extended the benefits of Canadian copyright to Bahrain. If, however, the Bahrain artist created the painting while residing in Berlin, the artist would acquire Canadian copyright because at the time of creation of the work the artist was resident in Germany, one of the member countries of the Berne Convention.

The second condition concerns published works. For copyright to exist in a published work, it must have been published within the Commonwealth, in one of the countries that has adhered to the Berne Convention, or in one of the countries to which Canada has extended benefits under the Copyright Act.

Most industrialized countries are members of the Berne Convention, and, therefore, their citizens and subjects are entitled to Canadian copyright for their works wherever created. The United States only recently adhered to the Berne Convention. Prior to that time, copyright was extended to U.S. citizens and subjects and to works first published in the United States because the United States was one of the foreign countries Canada extended its copyright laws to.

2. Who the author is

In the field of visual arts, the identification of the author of the work — that is, the artist — is not usually a difficult task. Under copyright law, the author is the person who gives a work original character. This is usually the creator of the work. The author is not, therefore, the technician who merely follows the artist's directions in creating the work. The author of a limited edition of prints is not, except in the most unusual of cases, the print maker, but instead, is usually the person who created the engraving or the drawing from which the engraving was derived. Note, however, the exception discussed below concerning authorship of photographs (see section **b. 5.**)

3. Which works are protected

Not all works are protected by copyright. Only works that fall within the definitions of artistic, dramatic, literary, and musical work, or devices that mechanically reproduce sound, are protected. Much contemporary artistic endeavor includes works that fall within one or more of these categories. In fact, a single work can attract multiple copyrights that may be owned, licensed, and otherwise dealt with by separate copyright owners. (See section **b.** of this chapter.)

Generally speaking, most traditional works of fine art constitute artistic works under the Copyright Act and are protected. Artistic work is defined in the act as "including paintings, drawings, photographs, engravings, sculptures, and works of artistic craftsmanship." Note that the definition is inclusive, not exclusive, and that neither the term "artistic" nor "craftsmanship" is defined in the act.

Dramatic works, of interest to performance artists, are also defined in an inclusive way. They include works intended for recitation or entertainment that involve scenic arrangement or an acting form, choreographic works, and what is known as "cinematographic productions" that are original.

In a minor amendment to the Copyright Act in 1993, the definition of "musical work" was changed to protect any work that is a combination of one or more of melody, harmony, or rhythm. The 1993 amendment removed the earlier restriction that confined musical works to combinations of melody or harmony that were reproduceuced graphically or in writing.

Copyright also applies to literary works, which include works of fiction or non-fiction, compilations, and computer programs. Therefore, artwork that uses text may be protected by copyright as both literary works and artistic works.

An underlying requirement for each of the categories is that the work be fixed in a permanent way: in writing, in graphic presentation, recorded on film or videotape, or otherwise. It must be possible to identify with certainty the work to which the copyright applies.

4. The rights included

Copyright is not a right to receive financial compensation for the creation of an artistic work. The rights conveyed by copyright may, however, be used or exploited by the owner to secure economic reward. Copyright includes what is referred to as "a bundle of rights." The principal rights are the following:

(a) The exclusive right to produce or reproduce the entire work or a substantial part of the work in its original form or in any other material form. For example, the reproduction of a painting in another painting or in another form such as a photograph or video would be within this right of the copyright owner.

(b) The exclusive right to perform the work or a substantial part of the work in public. This would be the principal right for performance artists.

(c) For an unpublished work, the exclusive right to publish the work or any substantial part of the work. Publication would likely occur on the sale of slides of a painting to members of the public with the consent of the copyright owner, for example.

(d) The exclusive right to convert a non-dramatic work, including an artistic work, into a dramatic work by performing the work in public. This right may also be of interest to performance artists.

(e) The exclusive right to communicate the work to the public by telecommunication, such as radio or television. This right includes the broadcast by television of a video record of a painter's exhibition.

(f) The exclusive right to present an artistic work at a public exhibition for a purpose other than for the sale or hire of the work. (Note: the right of public exhibition applies only to artistic works created after June 8, 1988 with the exception of maps, charts, plans, and films that do not contain dramatic elements. The scope of this right is not entirely clear. It likely includes an exhibition in a museum or gallery, but it is uncertain whether it extends to the display of a work in a public place such as the lobby of an office tower to which the public is invited or has access. There is currently a debate among artists and public galleries about whether a fee should be paid to the artist for the display of a work in a public exhibition and the amount of any payment.)

(g) The exclusive right to authorize the doing of any acts that are within the rights of copyright is independent from the possession or ownership of the artwork. For example, a sculptor, on creating a piece, owns the sculpture itself and would likely also have possession of the sculpture. The sculptor can transfer possession of the sculpture by loaning it to a friend and ownership by selling the sculpture. However, the copyright in the sculpture is still held by the sculptor unless he or she assigns the copyright in a written agreement.

5. Who owns copyright

The author is generally the copyright owner. One exception to this rule applies to works made by an employee during the course of employment. Unless agreed otherwise, the employer, and not the employee, is the copyright owner. There are specific exceptions for portraits, engravings, and photographs, which are discussed in section **b.** of this chapter.

One of the virtues of the Copyright Act is the flexibility provided for the assignment or licensing of copyright. The owner of copyright may assign or license all or part of the copyright as a bundle of separate rights. The assignment or licence may be for the whole of Canada, or just for certain areas. It can be for the entire unexpired term of the copyright, or for any lesser term.

For example, a photographer may assign to a person the right to reproduce a photograph within British Columbia with the ability to sell such right to a third party. The photographer may then convey to a second person a licence to permit the use of the photograph in the production of a video in

Ontario; and to a public museum in Nova Scotia the photographer may license the right to exhibit the photograph at an exhibition for one year.

Through careful management of the bundle of copyrights, an artist can maximize the economic return for the use of his or her work by others. The only restriction on an assignment or grant of licence of copyright is that it must be in writing, signed by the owner of the copyright or his or her authorized agent.

6.   The term of copyright

Copyright has a long life. Generally, copyright comes into existence on the creation of the work and continues for 50 years after the death of the artist. If a literary, dramatic, or musical work or an engraving of the artist has not been published at the time of the author's death, copyright extends until publication and for 50 years after that. There are additional rights for dramatic and musical works first performed in public posthumously.

A number of exceptions to these general rules are discussed in the section **b.** of this chapter.

7.   The estate pitfall

The Copyright Act contains a little-known pitfall for anyone who wishes to acquire copyright from an artist. If, before he or she dies, the artist assigns or licenses the copyright in a work, that assignment or licence expires 25 years after the artist's death. The copyright then reverts to the artist's estate for the unexpired term of copyright, which in most cases is an additional 25 years. This applies even if there is an agreement to the contrary, but it does *not* apply if the author grants copyright of the work in his or her will.

This provision can reduce the amount a person may pay to the artist to acquire copyright (while the artist is alive) and may therefore limit the artist's ability to fully exploit the economic potential of his or her works. Further revision of

Canada's copyright laws may well repeal this provision. Until this happens, artists and those who seek to acquire copyright must be aware of this provision and adjust their contractual arrangements to take the provision into account.

8. Publication

The existence and term of copyright for certain works depends on whether the work is published. The Copyright Act defines "publication" as the issue of copies of the work to the public. As with many of the provisions of the Copyright Act, there are many exceptions which will be discussed in section **b.** of this chapter.

The concept of publication is difficult to apply to works of art. It is not common for a painter to create copies of a painting and to sell or otherwise distribute those copies. It is more common, however, for a painter to consent to a reproduction in a print, slide, or postcard for sale at a museum or gallery shop concurrent with the exhibition of the painting. It is likely that the sale or distribution of these prints, slides, or postcards amounts to publication of the painting. The same would likely apply to the reproduction of the painting in a catalogue of an exhibition that is sold or distributed to the public with the painter's consent.

If first publication of a work takes place in a country to which the Copyright Act does not extend, then copyright in Canada is lost. For example, if a Canadian artist exhibits a work in Bahrain, and for the first time consents to the reproduction of the work in a postcard distributed to the public in Bahrain, the artist will lose Canadian copyright because Bahrain does not adhere to the Berne Convention and the benefit of Canadian copyright has not been extended to Bahrain.

Artists who exhibit works abroad and who permit reproductions of the work to be distributed or sold should ensure that the country in which the reproductions are first distributed or sold adheres to the Berne Convention or is otherwise a country to which Canada extends the benefit of copyright.

9. Registration

It is a relatively simple matter for an owner of copyright to register with the Copyright Office, which is located in Ottawa/Hull. Copyright may be registered in both published and unpublished works. It is not necessary to furnish the Copyright Office with a reproduction of the work in order to register copyright.

Registration of copyright offers only limited benefits, however, and these benefits largely relate to proof of the existence and ownership of copyright in case of a lawsuit. Copyright may be registered at any time and in most instances, there is no need for an artist to register.

Artists can also register assignments and licences of copyright with the Copyright Office, regardless of whether the copyright itself is registered, and there is substantial benefit in doing so. If an artist assigns or licenses copyright to a work to one person, and at a later date assigns or grants a conflicting licence to a second person, the person who registers the assignment with the Copyright Office will be the one entitled under law to the assignment.

For example, suppose an artist assigns all copyright in a painting to her dealer, and then later purports to assign all copyright in the same painting to a museum. If the museum has no knowledge of the previous assignment and it registers its assignment before the dealer, the museum will secure the assignment. In effect, the museum, by registering its assignment before the dealer, has defeated the rights that the dealer initially acquired. The dealer may, depending on the circumstances, have a claim against the artist, but even if successful, the dealer will not be able to secure the copyright.

10. Infringement of copyright

Generally, it is an infringement of copyright to do anything without permission that only the copyright owner may do. It is, therefore, an infringement of copyright to publish an un-published work or to reproduce a substantial part of a work even in another format without first obtaining the consent of the copyright owner. It would not be an infringement of copyright to reproduce a detail of a work unless the detail is considered a substantial part of the work.

It is an infringement of copyright for someone to import into Canada a foreign-made copy of a work for the purposes of selling, leasing, distributing, or exhibiting the work in Canada if he or she knows that the making of the copy in Canada would infringe copyright. For example, suppose an artist grants copyright in one of her paintings to a Hong Kong company to make and sell copies of the painting as posters. The licence is confined to Hong Kong and the artist retains all rights to make copies of the painting in Canada. Sub-sequently, a dealer purchases the posters in Hong Kong and imports them into Canada for resale to his customers. By doing so, the dealer is infringing the artist's copyright both by importing the posters and by selling them — if he knew at the time of importation or sale that the making of the posters in Canada would be a copyright infringement.

There are two general exemptions from copyright in-fringement that are relevant to artists' works. The first is "fair dealing" of a work for purposes of private study, research, criticism, review, or newspaper summary. This exemption, of critical importance to educators, students, and journalists, is not well understood.

The scope of the activities that constitute fair dealing is not known. It is probably not an infringement for a journalist to reproduce a portion of an artist's work in a newspaper review. It is less certain whether the journalist would be entitled to reproduce the entire work unless it was necessary to do so in order to effectively criticize or review.

Similar questions arise for educators. One thing is clear, however. It is an infringement of copyright for a teacher to make multiple copies of an artist's work for distribution to students in a classroom, even if the intended use of the copies is for the private study of students.

The second exemption from infringement applies to an artist who creates a work, but who no longer owns copyright on that work. The artist may re-use any mould, cast, sketch, model, or study used to create the first work, but only if in doing so he or she does not repeat the main design of the first work.

(**Note:** there is a third exemption from infringement of copyright relevant to sculptors and craftspersons, and that is discussed in section **b.** 2 and 7 of this chapter.)

11.   Remedies

If someone's copyright has been infringed, there are extensive remedies available under the law. The owner of copyright is entitled both to a monetary award for damages as well as a share of the profits made by the infringer that the court concludes is just. Furthermore, an infringing copy of a work is considered the property of the owner of copyright and a court can order that the copy be turned over to him or her. If the infringer is not in a position to deliver the work to the copyright owner, he or she has to pay an amount that represents its value.

Apart from financial entitlement, in appropriate circumstances a court will grant an injunction to restrain the continuation of the infringing activities. In most successful cases, the copyright owner is also entitled to an award of costs, although these are generally not high enough to reimburse the actual legal costs incurred.

It is critically important for artists to begin legal proceedings in any copyright infringement case within three years of the infringement. After three years, if no proceedings have begun, the copyright owner loses any claim to monetary compensation.

12. Collectives

Canada's copyright legislation provides a mechanism for the collective administration of certain rights of copyright. The mechanism applies to the collective administration of performance rights in dramatic-musical or musical works. This has facilitated the creation of collectives that have for many years successfully operated to secure, on behalf of their members, royalties for the performance in public of musical works.

The copyright collective for such rights is known as the Society of Composers, Authors and Music Publishers of Canada (SOCAN). SOCAN was created in March, 1990 as a result of a merger of the prior collectives, Composers, Authors and Publishers Association of Canada (CAPAC), and Performing Rights Organization of Canada (PROCAN).

The 1988 amendment to the Copyright Act facilitated the creation of additional collectives, referred to as licensing bodies. Now, VIS-ART Copyright, Inc. operates as a collective to administer reproduction rights of works of fine art. VIS-ART represents a repertoire of well-known domestic and international artists, both alive and deceased. Picasso is one of the artists within the VIS-ART repertoire. VIS-ART will undertake all the necessary arrangements for the reproduction of its artists' works in posters, slides, and catalogues, and will return to the artists the royalties received minus VIS-ART's administration fee.

Steps have also been taken by Canadian Artists Representation (CARFAC) to establish and administer a collective for artists' exhibition rights. This collective has been less successful in operating as a viable business entity, largely because exhibition rights apply only to certain artistic works created after June 8, 1988. Over time, as more works include exhibition rights, the viability of this collective will increase.

If an artist elects to join a collective, he or she is obliged to assign or license the rights administered by the collective. The collective grants all licences or permissions concerning the artist's works that are within the scope of its mandate. The artist then receives royalties from the collective (less an amount to cover administration costs) for any use of his or her work.

13. Joint versus collective authorship

The Copyright Act distinguishes between works of joint authorship and collective works. A work of joint authorship is a work in which two or more authors contribute to the creation and their respective contributions are amalgamated in such a way that their contributions cannot be separately identified. On the other hand, a collective work constitutes a work in which more than one author has contributed distinct parts. An example of a collective work is a song for which one musician wrote the lyrics and the other composed the music. Another musical work may constitute a work of joint authorship if both musicians contributed to either or both of the lyrics and music in a collaborative way so that the contributions of each could not be identified.

The term of copyright is different for joint and collective authorships. For a joint authorship, copyright lasts for 50 years after the death of the last of the authors to die. For a collective work, copyright of the contributions expires 50 years from the death of each of the respective contributors. That is, the copyright of the lyrics of the song would expire 50 years after the death of the lyricist, but the copyright of the music would expire 50 years after the death of the composer.

14. Moral rights

Canada's copyright laws create two moral rights. The first, known internationally as the right of paternity, conveys to the artist the right to have his or her name associated with the work as the author. The second is the right of integrity in the artist's work, meaning the right to prevent the distortion, mutilation, or other modification of the work and to prevent the use of the work in conjunction with a product, service, cause, or institution.

The right of integrity is infringed only if the honor and reputation of the author is prejudiced. For paintings, sculptures, or engravings, prejudice to the artist's honor in reproduction is assumed. So although it would be an infringement to deface an artist's painting, it would not be an infringement to deface a photograph, unless the photographer could also establish that his or her honor was prejudiced. Establishing this prejudice in a court of law could be very difficult.

The moral rights of an artist are completely independent from copyright, although they subsist for the same term as copyright in a work. An artist may assign copyright but not moral rights. Moral rights are not, therefore, capable of being exploited in the same way as the economic right of copyright.

It is possible, however, for an artist to *waive* his or her moral rights. An oral waiver can be effective, but it is advisable that any waiver be in writing. A waiver of the moral rights of the creator may be entirely appropriate for certain works created in a commercial context. For example, there may be numerous employees of a company who participate in the creation of computer software, each of whom would normally be entitled to claim authorship and the moral right of paternity. But it may be unwieldy and commercially undesirable to display the names of all the employees involved. The employer may, therefore, be fully justified in requiring its employees to waive their moral right of paternity in works created during the course of employment.

One of the most noted examples of infringement of an artist's moral right of integrity occurred when the Toronto Eaton Centre displayed Michael Snow's sculpture of a flock of geese. Without authorization, the Toronto Eaton Centre arranged for Christmas decorations to be hung from the necks of the geese. Michael Snow took exception to the modification of his sculpture and secured a court order requiring the Eaton Centre to remove the decorations based on a claim of infringement of his moral right of integrity. At the time of the lawsuit, there was no provision for financial relief for the infringement of moral rights, but now a court may grant damages or an accounting of the profits made by the defendant through the infringement.

15. International copyright

For many Canadian artists, copyright is critical not only in Canada but abroad. For these artists the Berne Convention provides extended protection.

The Berne Convention requires member countries to enact copyright legislation which treats their nationals no more favorably than nationals of other member countries. In addition, the Berne Convention requires that member countries protect artistic works by copyright without the necessity of registration of copyright or attending to other formalities, such as the use of a copyright symbol or notice.

As most countries of the industrialized world are members of the Berne Convention, Canadian artists can, with some comfort, know that their works are protected by copyright in most places to the same extent as if they were nationals of those countries. To determine the copyright laws of any specific country, however, it is necessary to examine the legislation of that country.

b. HOW THE LAW APPLIES TO VARIOUS ART FORMS

1. Paintings and drawings (excluding portraits)

Paintings and drawings are included within the definition of artistic work, but are not themselves defined in the act.

Neither artistic merit nor aesthetic taste is relevant in determining whether copyright exists in paintings or drawings. A drawing intended by its creator to appeal to the aesthetic senses is, therefore, equally capable of protection by copyright.

Traditionally, paintings were made on stretched canvas over wood frames, on board, or as frescoes. Contemporary art has redefined the traditional notion of a painting. In the seventies, Betty Goodwin created unstructured tarpaulins or canvases that were intended to be loosely hung from the wall or other surface. In addition, she created works consisting of vests applied to a board. More recently John Heward has created rayons intended to be draped from a wall or ceiling. These works are protected either as paintings or as works falling generally within the inclusive definition of artistic works.

The use of text is not uncommon in contemporary painting and drawing. The works of Greg Curnoe and Charles Gagnon are just two examples of paintings in which text is prominent. For such works, the paintings as a whole are protected by copyright as artistic works and the texts may be protected separately as literary works. The owner of the copyright might, therefore, be able to prevent the unauthorized reproduction of the text that does not in any way resemble the painting as a whole. There is, however, a limitation on the extent to which text may be protected by copyright. It is unlikely that the mere title of a work or a short common phrase would be protected by copyright.

A painting or drawing is published only when it is reproduced in multiple copies with the authorization of the copyright owner. Public exhibition is not publication of the work.

Copyright in an unpublished painting or drawing expires 50 years after the artist's death. The copyright cannot extend beyond that time even if, after the author's death, the painting or drawing is published. Note that this is contrary to the general principles discussed above that apply to dramatic, literary, and musical works.

2. Sculpture

Sculpture is also a traditional field of artistic endeavor protected by copyright as an artistic work. As with paintings and drawings, sculpture is not defined specifically in the Copyright Act.

There are two peculiarities to copyright in sculptures. First, a photograph or engraving of a sculpture does not amount to publication of the sculpture. Publication occurs if the artist makes or authorizes the making for sale of either an edition of the sculpture or, perhaps, drawings that depict the sculpture.

The second peculiarity applies to sculptures permanently displayed in public places or in buildings. It is not an infringement of copyright to make or publish paintings, drawings, engravings, or photographs of such sculptures. It is, however, an infringement to photograph a sculpture on display for sale in a commercial gallery without the permission of the copyright owner.

3. Portraits

Portraits that are paintings or drawings (i.e., not photographs) are covered by a particular exception under the copyright law. Generally, copyright is held by the creator of the portrait. However, if a portrait is commissioned by someone, that person owns the copyright, subject to any agreement to the contrary.

A portrait artist who wishes to retain copyright must, therefore, be sure to enter into an agreement for any commissioned work. The agreement should clearly state that the copyright remains with the artist.

4. Engravings

The Copyright Act defines engravings to include etchings, lithographs, woodcuts, and prints, but it excludes photographs. Generally an artist who creates an engraving is the copyright owner.

An Inuit artist may, for example, create a drawing that is used by a member of a collective to make a plate for reproduction as a lithograph. The artist would be the copyright owner in this case. If the person who made the plate embellished upon the artist's drawing and therefore contributed artistic elements to the lithograph, a separate copyright would arise in the lithograph.

It is also possible, however, that the lithograph would be a work of joint authorship if the separate contributions could not be discerned. If so, the artist who drew the drawing and the member of the collective who created the plate would jointly be the owners of copyright.

If an engraving is commissioned, the ownership may be uncertain. If the plate or other original of the engraving is commissioned and money is paid for it, the person giving the commission would be the copyright owner, subject to any agreement to the contrary. In the above example of the Inuit lithograph, if a person commissioned the lithograph and not the drawing on which the lithograph was based, the artist who created the drawing would own the copyright of the drawing and the person who commissioned the lithograph would own the copyright of the lithograph. The rights of one of these individuals as against the other would be uncertain.

One aspect of the law applicable to engravings that *is* certain is the term of copyright after the death of the artist. Engravings are the only category of artistic work that if first published posthumously, extend copyright for a period of 50 years from *publication*, rather than from the date of death of the author.

5. Photographs

Photographs include photolithographs and any works produced by a process analogous to photography. At the time that Canada's Copyright Act was enacted, making a photograph involved the creation of a negative. Instant camera technology was invented many years later. Today, Polaroid photographs are taken without creating a negative. Are those photographs protected by the Copyright Act?

Surprisingly, it is likely that our courts would interpret the Copyright Act to *exclude* copyright protection for a Polaroid print as a photograph, but would find it to be protected as an artistic work. The difference in the protection is discussed below.

The Copyright Act contains peculiarities about the authorship and the term of copyright protection for photographs. The person who owns the negative at the time it is made is deemed to be the author of the print made from the negative. Therefore, a photographer who borrows equipment will not necessarily own the copyright in the photographs taken. Instead, the person who loaned the equipment and who owned the negative at the time that the photograph was taken would own copyright. However, if the photographer borrows Polaroid equipment, there is no negative, and the photographer, not the owner of the equipment, owns the copyright.

The term of copyright for a photograph is 50 years from the date of making the original negative, *not* 50 years from the death of the author. But the term of copyright for a Polaroid print is 50 years from the date of the death of the photographer.

A commissioned photograph is subject to the same provisions of the copyright law as a commissioned portrait or engraving (discussed above.) If the negative from which the photograph is made is commissioned, the person commissioning it is the owner of the copyright, subject to any agreement to the contrary. Although it is common for photographs to be commissioned, it is less common for a negative to be commissioned.

6. Collage

A collage may be a collection of extracts from media, photographs, drawings, or other items that are assembled into a free-standing sculpture or wall piece. The artistic creation involves the collection and arrangement of the individual components of the collage. Alan Harding McKay recently exhibited collages consisting of photographs, taken both by himself and other photographers, and other materials from media depicting the civil strife in Somalia. In addition to those components, the artist combined some of his own drawings. The artistic creation involved the selection, arrangement, and display of the individual elements.

A collage is likely protected as a compilation, which is one of the works listed in the Copyright Act as a literary work. Therefore, protection in a collage would be confined to the *collection and arrangement* of items or images and would not extend to the *individual* items or images. Accordingly, although Alan Harding McKay may hold copyright in his collages of Somalia, he does not hold copyright in the individual photographs of the other photographers' works he used within the collage. In other words, he would not be able to prohibit someone else from reproducing those photographs individually.

A word of caution to artists creating collages: Unless you obtain the authorization of the owner of the copyright in individual images and text used in a collage, you may not be able to reproduce the collage without infringing copyright in the individual elements. Furthermore, if you were to use someone else's painting or engraving in creating a collage, any distortion or modification of the painting or engraving could constitute an infringement of the moral right of the artist. Collage artists should always consult with the copyright holders and obtain appropriate permissions.

48

7. Crafts

The Copyright Act protects works of artistic craftsmanship as artistic works. The act does not, however, define works of artistic craftsmanship. Crafts such as ceramics, jewelry, carvings, and fine furniture might well constitute works of artistic craftsmanship and, therefore, be protected by the law.

A work of artistic craftsmanship must have an artistic element. The courts have been obliged to address aesthetics in determining what constitutes artistic craftsmanship, but because our courts try to refrain from being arbiters on matters of artistic and aesthetic taste, they have looked at the author's intent. If the author intended to apply skill and taste to produce a work that would have a substantial appeal to aesthetic taste, then the object is likely to be construed as a work of artistic craftsmanship.

For example, the courts refused to consider a series of colored rods of different lengths created to teach children mathematics as a work of artistic craftsmanship. The court concluded that the appeal to the aesthetic senses was not an important object for which the rods were created, and a claim for copyright in the rods failed.

If a craft item is a useful article, such as a ceramic bowl, other limitations apply. If the artistic design consists only of the shape and configuration of the bowl and the artist makes (or authorizes the making of) 50 or more copies of the bowl, it is likely that someone else would be able to reproduce the work without infringing copyright.

Crafts are frequently reproduced in quantity, and if that quantity is more than 50, in most cases they must be protected as an industrial design. Industrial Designs are protected by registering with the Industrial Design Office in Ottawa/Hull and only by applying within one year of showing the design to the public.

8. Film and video

Increasingly, contemporary artists choose to express their creativity in film, and more recently, in video. Unfortunately, there is no separate category for audiovisual works as there is in the United States. At the time the Canadian legislation was drafted, "talking pictures" were yet to be developed and marketed, and video technology was not even in its infancy. As a result, the full scope of copyright protection for film and video is uncertain, and therefore, unsatisfactory.

(a) Film

Film is primarily protected under the Copyright Act as a dramatic work, which includes cinematograph productions. The act defines cinematograph to include any work made by a process analogous to cinematography. To be protected as a cinematograph production a film must consist of a sequence of photographs.

A further condition must also be met: the arrangement, acting form, or combination of incidents represented in the film must give the film an original character. For example, a film of nature with no editing would not be protected because there would be no original character. Similarly, a film made of a live football game would not be protected. In this case, the producer has nothing to do with the scenic arrangements or the acting form of the players who participated in the game.

Copyright for a film extends to the dramatic elements, being the arrangement, acting form, or combination of incidents. The film would have all the rights of copyright discussed above including the right to broadcast on a television or cable network. The copyright owner is generally the producer of the film, subject to any agreement to the contrary.

If a visual artist films an unedited series of events in real life, or if for the other reasons discussed above, the film is not protected as a dramatic work, copyright still protects the film,

50

but only to the extent that it consists of a series of photographs (see above). This means that the copyright would extend for 50 years from the taking of the film, rather than 50 years from the death of the producer, and the person who owned the negative when the film was taken would be the copyright owner rather than the producer.

A well-known example of such a film is Michael Snow's *La Régione Centrale* from 1970. In the film, Snow set a camera to take, in slow speed, a 360-degree view of the landscape in northern Quebec. The film does not contain any reference to the human form and would not be protected as a dramatic work. The copyright would, therefore, be confined to the series of photographs that make up the film and would extend only for a period of 50 years from the actual filming.

Copyright in a film protected as a dramatic work accords the owner of the copyright the sole right to perform the work in public. This would not, however, likely be the case for a film without an audio component that is only protected as a series of photographs. Furthermore, there is no right to present the film at a public exhibition. Exhibition rights are specifically excluded for cinematographic films protected as a photograph. This position is inconsistent because a photograph itself attracts exhibition rights, but a cinematographic film that is protected as a photograph does not.

The script of a film would be separately protected by copyright as a literary work, and any musical score would be separately protected as a musical work. The author who created the script generally owns the copyright in the script and the composer owns the copyright in the musical score. These individuals might be different than the producer of the film who would likely be the copyright owner if the film is protected as a dramatic work.

Another complexity arises if the film depicts scenery that has been created by the producer or another visual artist. The scenery may be separately protected by copyright as an artistic work. Furthermore, a film may also be protected as a contrivance by means of which sound may be mechanically reproduced. All that would be required for this protection would be for the film to be capable of being used to reproduce sound. Any film with a soundtrack would, therefore, qualify. However, the protection would only extend to the audio portion of the film and would be restricted to the sole right to reproduce the film or any substantial part of it in any material form. The rights would not include, for example, the right to communicate the film by telecommunication.

Because of the complex nature of the copyright that may arise in cinematographic films, if a number of individuals are involved in creating a film, it is common to define the rights of the various contributors by agreement.

(b) Video

Canada's copyright laws leave video artists in a state of great uncertainty concerning the existence, extent, and ownership of copyright in their video productions.

A video is not protected as a cinematograph production because it consists of a series of electronic impulses, and not a sequence of photographs. Instead, it is possible that our courts would conclude that video would fall within the general scope of a dramatic work, but only if the scenic arrangement, acting form, or combination of incidents create a dramatic element. Given the current state of the law, it is unlikely that a video that does not contain a script of words and an arrangement of incidents would be protected as a dramatic work.

If a video is *not* protected by copyright as a dramatic work, certain features may still be covered in a manner similar to cinematographic films. The script may be protected as a literary work, the musical score as a musical work, and the entire video as a contrivance by means of which sound may be mechanically produced. In the last case, the copyright would not likely extend beyond the audio portion of the video.

If a video *is* protected as a dramatic work, the video artist, if he or she is the producer of the video, would be the copyright owner.

Hopefully, the next phase of copyright revision will include the protection of video specifically within a new category of work. Only an amendment to the Copyright Act will make the rights of video artists more certain.

9. Multi-media works and installations

The complexities of copyright also apply to multi-media works and installations. A multi-media work, as the name implies, includes components from different media, usually including film or video. In general terms, an installation is a work "installed" for a limited time at a specific location. Such a work is usually made of a combination of ready-made objects. The combination, which may also include video or film, is intended to illustrate a concept developed by the artists.

In addition to whatever copyright may subsist in the film or video components of a multi-media work or installation, additional sculptural components, paintings, drawings, or photographs may also attract separate copyright as artistic works. The scope of the copyright in these additional components is governed by the law as discussed in various sections above.

The overall composition of a multi-media work and an installation can also be protected as a compilation. As with a collage (see above), the copyright extends to the selection or arrangement of the individual items, but not to any individual element or component of the work. The copyright does not, however, extend to protect any video component, if one exists. To stop someone from reproducing any component, the artist must rely on any separate copyright that may exist in the component as if the component were a separate work.

10. Public art

Public art is usually sculpture, such as the works of Melvin
Charney and Al McWilliams, or works incorporated into a
building, such as the work of Calatrava in BCE Place in
Toronto. Under the Copyright Act, it is not an infringement
of copyright to make paintings, drawings, engravings, or
photographs of a sculpture or work of artistic craftsmanship
permanently situated in a public place or building. Curiously,
however, if the public art is *not* a sculpture or a work of artistic
craftsmanship (e.g., a photograph), then making a painting,
drawing, engraving, or photograph would amount to copyright infringement unless, of course, it was made with the
consent of the copyright owner.

Public art raises a unique issue regarding the artist's
moral rights. It is an infringement of an artist's moral right of
integrity to distort, mutilate, or modify a painting, sculpture,
or engraving. This does not include changing the location of
a work or the means by which the work is displayed. It would
not be an infringement of the artist's moral rights to move a
sculpture from one public square to another. However, if the
site contributed artistically to the work itself, the artist would
have grounds for arguing that any change in location would
infringe his or her moral right of integrity.

Works of public art, especially those subjected to the
vicissitudes of the weather, may deteriorate over time.
There is no obligation on the owner of the work, under the
law relating to moral rights, to maintain the work and
protect the work from deterioration. Any obligation of this
kind should be the subject of detailed contractual terms
between the artist and owner. (See chapter 8 for more on
maintaining public artwork.)

It is a more difficult issue when a work deteriorates to the
point that the owner wishes to destroy it. Any destruction
would constitute an infringement of the artist's moral rights.
In such circumstances, the owner should either return the

work to the artist or obtain the artist's consent to any destruction.

11. Conceptual works

Jana Sterbak has attracted considerable attention for her meat dress exhibited recently at the National Gallery of Canada. The work consists of pieces of raw meat sewn together in a particular way to form a dress. The artistic component and originality lies in the concept of the meat dress more than in the style of the dress.

It is difficult to apply copyright in a meaningful way to conceptual works. A fundamental principal of copyright law is that it protects the form of a work, but not the idea behind it. In the case of Jana Sterbak's meat dress, copyright would protect the particular design as an artistic work, but would not prevent another person from making a dress using meat in a different design. The result denies Sterbak of any meaningful copyright. The only protection she would have would be moral support and perhaps, therefore, protection conveyed by the artistic community and the community's collective disapproval if someone else tried to benefit from the original artistic creation by displaying another meat dress devoid of independent artistic creation.

12. Artist collectives

A number of artist collectives have produced creative and challenging works over the last 20 years. Two noted collectives are General Idea and Fast Wurms. Many works of these art collectives are, under copyright law, true collective works. The collective collaborates in the artistic endeavor in such a way that the contribution of each individual merges in the whole and cannot be discerned from the completed work.

As indicated earlier in this chapter, the term of copyright in a work of joint authorship created by an artist collective extends for 50 years after the death of the last member of the collective — even though the collective itself may cease to exist on the death of any one member. Each member of a collective work has a right as a joint owner of copyright. The law is unsettled over the issue of how copyright passes on the death of one of the members of the collective. It may pass to other members of the collective, or instead, to the estate of the deceased. Likely, the courts would decide the former.

If the contribution of each member of the artist collective is identifiable, then the work would be considered a collective work, and the copyright on each contribution would extend for 50 years from the death of the contributing member of the collective.

To obtain an assignment or licence of copyright of a joint work of a collective, each member of the collective should provide a written assignment or licence. One member alone cannot grant an exclusive licence because he or she cannot, unless authorized by the other members by contract, restrain other members of the collective from also dealing with the copyright.

13.   Performance art

Over the last 20 years, a number of artists practiced performance art, and they would perform themselves or authorize others to perform their work over a period of time.

To attract copyright protection, a performance must first be fixed in writing or in another tangible way, such as recorded on video, in order to identify the work with precision. An impromptu performance that relies on improvisation and that is not documented or recorded is not protected.

A performance may be protected as a dramatic work, but only to the extent that the work contains a scenic arrangement, acting form, or combination of incidents that gives the work an original character, or to the extent that it is a choreographic work. (A choreographic work is defined by the Copyright Act as including any work of choreography whether or not it has a story line.) Copyright may also extend to any script as a literary work, to any score as a musical work, and perhaps to any scenery or props as artistic works.

14. Computer-based works

The development of new technologies provides opportunities for new contemporary art practices. A recent example is computer technology, and in particular, computer programs. Contemporary art may include the use of a computer program by the viewer, perhaps in an interactive capacity, or the use of the program by the artist to generate a unique computer output such as a printout. Contemporary artists, including Stacey Spiegal of Toronto, have created such works using computer programs.

The amendments to the Copyright Act in 1988 specifically included computer programs within the definition of literary works and, therefore, extended copyright protection to them.

If the work of art is the program itself, it is protected by copyright as a literary work. If the work of art is the output of a computer, the output would likely be protected as an artistic work, and if the output includes text, it is also protected as a literary work. In the latter case, the computer is merely being used as a tool, like a paint brush, to create the work of art.

There may be certain instances in which the artistic endeavor involves the use of a programmed computer by the artist or a member of the public to produce a random computer output. In this case, copyright law has difficulty in determining the first owner of copyright. The owner may be the artist who conceived the artistic endeavor, the person who programmed the computer, or the artist or member of the public who produced the computer output. In these circumstances, the artist should establish his or her claim to copyright by agreement in writing with all parties involved.

c. CONCLUSION

The creative mind has no boundary. Artists seek to extend and redefine experience through art practices that frequently involve diverse means including emerging technologies. Unfortunately, Canada's copyright laws have failed to keep up with both developments in the creative arts and the new technologies. The Copyright Act has for many years been outdated.

Although general rules in the act seek to establish and define principles, frequently these principles have no clearly consistent logical basis, or are subject to exceptions that are no longer appropriate. As a result, artists working in non-traditional media will be left in uncertainty as to the nature of their economic rights of copyright. This uncertainty will only be removed through legislative amendment, now unlikely for some time because of the highly contentious nature of copyright reform.

The prudent artist who practices in non-traditional media will seek to define right of copyright to the extent possible by agreement. The artist must seek to understand the complex and uncertain laws of copyright applicable to his or her practice. And artists should collectively advance the cause of copyright reform.

3

ART AND OBSCENITY LAW

*by Brian Blugerman**

The purpose of obscenity law is to control obscenity without unreasonably limiting artistic freedom. In this modern age, any assessment of the obscene character of art must take into account the value that is placed on freedom of expression in the Canadian Charter of Rights and Freedoms and the role creative expression plays in the development of our culture. Problems arise, however, in some cases when it may be difficult for a court or a customs officer to distinguish "art" from "obscenity," as both terms are difficult to define.

This ongoing dilemma was recognized by a U.S. court justice who aptly stated that "one man's vulgarity is another's lyric." Indeed, art historians can point to many works that society denounced as shocking and repulsive, only later to deem them artistic masterpieces. One example is the famous painting by Edouard Manet, *Le dejeuner sur l'herbe*, which caused an uproar in 1863 when it was first shown because of its casual depiction of nudity.

The concern that arises as a result of this confusion is that artists employing sexual themes or images cannot know with certainty whether their works will be found to be obscene. As a result, there is potential for a "chilling effect," or self-censorship, on their artistic expression. The possibility also exists that concerned gallery owners will cancel exhibitions of works that they feel may be found obscene by a court of law.

*This chapter was written with the assistance of Laurie May, student-at-law, Osler, Hoskin & Harcourt.

At times, these concerns may threaten to freeze the development of artistic expression in our society. While it is not possible to discuss in detail all of the difficult issues that arise in this area of the law, this chapter attempts to explain contemporary Canadian obscenity law as it relates to the field of visual arts.

a. THE INTERSECTION OF ART AND OBSCENITY

Which works of art will motivate the morality squad of a police force to investigate a particular exhibition? There is no easy answer to that question. It is, however, possible to identify three types of art that generally appear to invite the attention of the police.

First, whether they be publicly or privately owned, galleries may be investigated if they are involved in the public display of "a disgusting object or indecent show," which is an offence under the Criminal Code. Though never successfully prosecuted, the Isaacs Gallery in Toronto was charged in the early seventies for displaying the work of the artist Mark Prent of Montreal, whose art involves disturbing depictions of the human physical form.

The second kind of works of art that may occasion a visit from the police are those that portray sexual themes and, more specifically, works which feature as a dominant characteristic the "undue exploitation of sex." As discussed below, the "undue exploitation of sex" is a key element of obscenity as defined in the Criminal Code. It was the display of this kind of work that caused Dorothy Cameron, the owner and operator of a reputable commercial art gallery in Toronto, to be convicted by an Ontario court in 1966 for exposing obscene pictures to public view.

Finally, a third category of problematic works has been created by the recent enactment of child pornography provisions in the Criminal Code, which target explicit sexual depictions of persons who are, or appear to be, under the age of 18 (see discussion below).

Even if an artist or gallery owner is made aware of the kinds of art that may occasion an investigation by the police, some questions remain:

- Which works can actually be expected to lead to criminal convictions?

- When will a sculpture be seen to be a work of important cultural value and not a "disgusting object"?

- When will a performance artist be seen to be engaging in an inspiring artistic dance as opposed to an "indecent show"?

- How far can video artists explore sexual issues before they have crossed the invisible line?

- When will the display of graphic sexual portraits be seen to be provocative and not "obscene"?

The controversy surrounding the photographic work of the late American artist Robert Mapplethorpe exemplifies the confusion surrounding sexually explicit work in contemporary society. Mapplethorpe's portraits of men in homoerotic or sadomasochistic positions were seen by some to be classic photographs and by others to be pornographic and shocking by any standards.

b. THE EVOLUTION OF CANADIAN OBSCENITY LAW

By looking briefly at the history of obscenity law and the various tests that have been developed to determine whether a work of art will be deemed obscene, it is possible to better understand which artistic works will be tolerated and which might lead to a conviction under the criminal law.

1. When obscenity became a crime

The first attempt to criminalize obscenity in Canada took place in 1892, when Parliament enacted a provision regarding obscenity in the Criminal Code. This provision was based on moral precepts; it provided, among other things, that everyone is guilty of an offence who "knowingly, without lawful justification or excuse," makes, manufactures, sells, distributes, or circulates any obscene matter "tending to corrupt morals." As the Criminal Code did not include a definition of obscenity, courts in Canada followed the then famous test set out in the English case of *R. v. Hicklin*, which focused on "whether the tendency of the matter charged as obscenity is to deprave and corrupt those whose minds are open to immoral influence." This focus typified the English view of the courts as the guardians of public morals.

The obscenity provision was repealed in 1949 and a new section was substituted in which the words "knowingly, without lawful justification or excuse" were removed with respect to the making, printing, distributing, or circulating of obscene matter, or for possessing obscene matter for any of these purposes. Those words, however, continued to apply to, among other things, the selling of obscene matter or exposing of obscene matter to public view.

The current obscenity provision in the Criminal Code came into force in 1959 and is essentially the same as its predecessor, except that it sets out a statutory definition of obscenity. Under section 163(8) of the Criminal Code, "any publication a dominant characteristic of which is the undue exploitation of sex, or of sex and any one or more of the following subjects, namely, crime, horror, cruelty and violence, shall be deemed to be obscene."

This definition of obscenity replaced the *Hicklin* test, and, it was hoped, would bring obscenity law into the modern age. Indeed, in *Brodie v. The Queen,* a 1962 case which was the first to consider the current provision, the court held that the new definition provided a clean slate and had the effect of bringing in "an objective standard of obscenity." In that case, the court held that the book *Lady Chatterley's Lover*, by D.H. Lawrence, placed no more emphasis on the sexual theme than was required in its serious treatment, so there was no "undue exploitation of sex." The work was, therefore, not obscene.

2. Tests for obscenity

In order for a work or material to qualify as obscene under the Criminal Code, the exploitation of sex must not only be a dominant characteristic, but such exploitation must be "undue." Various tests have been formulated by the courts to help determine what is and is not "undue." The "community standards" test, applied in *Brodie* and in the 1985 case of *Towne Cinema Theatres Ltd. v. The Queen*, is an objective test of tolerance that requires the court to determine, based on a national standard, what the community would not tolerate. The test doesn't look at what Canadians would find acceptable for themselves, it looks at what they wouldn't tolerate *other* Canadians being exposed to. A second test states that material which exploits sex in a manner that is "degrading or dehumanizing" may also be undue.

The test of "internal necessities" or "artistic defense," first set out in the *Brodie* decision, is the last step in the analysis of whether the exploitation of sex is undue. A court will consider the work as a whole and assess whether the exploitation of sex plays a necessary role in advancing the plot or theme of the work. If so, the work is not obscene even if some of the material it contains would be obscene if it stood alone. In *R. v. Butler*, the 1992 Supreme Court of Canada decision dealing with the obscenity provisions in the Criminal Code, the view was expressed that "artistic merit rests at the heart of freedom of expression values and any doubt in this regard must be resolved in favor of freedom of expression."

3. The Butler decision: how it affects artists and the art community

The contemporary approach of the courts when dealing with obscenity law in Canada is set out in the recent *Butler* decision, in which the Supreme Court of Canada upheld the constitutionality of the obscenity provisions of the Criminal Code, stating that while section 163 infringes freedom of expression as guaranteed under the Canadian Charter of Rights and Freedoms, such infringement can be justified as reasonable in a free and democratic society. The decision is important because it affirmed that Parliament is entitled to criminalize the sale and distribution of certain pornographic materials.

Artists and gallery owners should look to *Butler* to assist them in predicting whether a work will be deemed to be obscene, as the decision contains a comprehensive attempt to clarify what is meant by the phrase "undue exploitation of sex." The interpretation of obscenity in the *Butler* decision is relevant for anyone involved in the creation or display of visual arts, although the facts in that case dealt specifically with the selling and renting of hard core videotapes and magazines as well as sexual paraphernalia.

The accused in *Butler* was charged with various counts of selling obscene material, possessing obscene material for the purpose of distribution or sale, and exposing obscene material to public view contrary to the Criminal Code. The appeal to the Supreme Court of Canada was confined to an examination of the constitutional validity of the definition of obscenity in subsection 163(8) of the Criminal Code, and once such provisions were upheld as valid, a new trial was directed on all of the charges. Gallery owners should take note of the charges laid in *Butler*, as they illustrate that not only is it a criminal offence to make such obscene materials, it is also a criminal offence to sell or expose such material to the public view or have such material in your possession for this purpose.

The *Butler* decision attempted to specify the relationship between the various tests of obscenity outlined above. In essence, it stated that courts will have to ascertain what the community will tolerate others being exposed to on the basis of the degree of harm that may flow from such exposure. In making this determination, the court held the following:

(a) the portrayal of sex coupled with violence will almost always constitute the undue exploitation of sex,

(b) explicit sex that is degrading or dehumanizing may be undue if the risk of harm is substantial, and

(c) explicit sex that is not violent and neither degrading nor dehumanizing will not be undue unless it employs children in its production.

4. The new child pornography law

Artists and gallery owners should also be aware that in 1993 the Criminal Code was amended to provide for the creation of a set of child pornography offences separate from the existing obscenity offences. The Criminal Code defines child pornography as —

(a) a photographic, film, video, or other visual representation that either

   (i) shows a person who is or is depicted as being under the age of 18 and is engaged in or is depicted as engaged in explicit sexual activity, or

   (ii) the dominant characteristic of which is the depiction, for a sexual purpose, of a sexual organ or the anal region of a person under the age of 18; or

(b) any written material or visual representation that advocates or counsels sexual activity with a person under the age of 18 that would be an offence under the Criminal Code.

Note that this definition includes representations of persons "depicted" as being under the age of 18 regardless of their actual age. Also significant is the fact that under this new provision, simple possession (i.e., possession that is not for commercial or distribution purposes) of such material is an offence punishable by imprisonment for up to five years.

From an artist's perspective, the new section is troubling because the meanings of a number of new phrases defining the offences are not clear. For example, an artist may not be able to predict whether a sculpture of young persons fondling each other will be seen to be "explicit sexual activity," or whether a drawing showing the breast of an adolescent girl will be seen to be the depiction of a "sexual organ."

It is not enough for an artist to believe that a person is 18 years or older. Anyone accused must show that he or she took all reasonable steps to ascertain the age of the person and to ensure that where the person was 18 years of age or more, he or she was not depicted as being under the age of 18. However, the child pornography provisions do contain a statutory artistic defense, which provides that the court shall find the accused not guilty if the representation that is alleged to constitute child pornography "has artistic merit or an educational, scientific, or medical purpose."

In December 1993, charges were laid against Toronto artist Eli Langer and an administrator of the Mercer Union Gallery under the new child pornography law, following Mercer Union's exhibition of artwork by Langer which depicted children in sexual situations. At the time of writing this book, the personal charges against Langer and the administrator of the gallery had been dropped — largely due to the vociferous outcry from the arts community and the media. But the Crown is still proceeding to have the artwork declared as child pornography. If the work is found to be pornography, it will be destroyed. This case has become a well-publicized example of the risks artists and gallery operators may run when they make or display explicit sexual depictions.

c. PLACE AND MANNER OF PRESENTATION

Theatre, gallery, and bookstore owners may feel they can avoid prosecution by presenting explicit material in a way that would reduce exposure to children or otherwise ensure that the target audience is carefully selected. For example, a theatre owner presenting a play involving nudity and simulated sex might put a warning sign at the door and on advertisements, and might prohibit attendance by people under 18. While these tactics might reduce the inclination of the police to lay charges, it is unclear whether they would help a theatre owner who was charged to escape conviction.

In *Towne Cinema Theatres Ltd. v. The Queen*, the majority of the court held that the place and manner of exhibition of the material (including the audience to whom it is directed) is irrelevant to whether the material is obscene. Similarly, the court in *Butler* was of the view that if material is not obscene under the established tests, it does not become so by reason of the person to whom it is or may be shown or exposed to, nor by reason of the place or manner in which it is shown. However, in the 1993 case of *R. v. Tremblay*, the Supreme Court seemed to take a different view, holding that the place and manner in which a sexually explicit dance is presented would affect a decision as to whether the dance is "indecent" by community standards. At the time of writing this question is unsettled.

d. PRIVATE COLLECTIONS

While gallery owners may risk being prosecuted for exhibiting obscene works of art to the public, owners of private collections need not be concerned about obscenity unless they invite the public to view their collections. Possession of obscene material is not an offence unless it is for the purpose of publication, distribution, circulation, or sale. However, as noted, the private possession of child pornography is an offence, whether or not such possession is for any other purpose. Artists should also bear in mind that the *making* of obscene works or child pornography is in itself a criminal offence and such works kept in a private collection (whether belonging to the artist or another person) may be seized to be used as evidence in a criminal prosecution.

e. CANADIAN CUSTOMS LAW

Anyone in the artistic community should also be aware that books, magazines, films, videos, recordings, and other artistic materials being imported into Canada are subject to seizure by Revenue Canada's Customs and Excise branch if they are deemed to be obscene or to be child pornography under the provisions of the Criminal Code. A Customs officer may determine the tariff classification of imported goods and, in so doing, may refer to published guidelines on obscenity.

If the officer determines that the material is prohibited, the decision can be challenged by the importer by requesting a redetermination by a tariff and values administrator. If the redetermination is unfavorable, the importer can request a further redetermination by the Deputy Minister of National Revenue for Customs and Excise. If the Deputy Minister's redetermination is also unfavorable, the importer may appeal the matter to a court of law.

On the other hand, if Customs does *not* prohibit material, that decision does not confer immunity from prosecution under the obscenity provisions of the Criminal Code.

An importer who is concerned that material is obscene can save time by seeking an advance ruling from Customs on the classification of materials. Publishers of a number of "men's magazines" regularly submit pre-publication copies for advance review, and sometimes delete material where Customs indicates that it is objectionable.

This practice of submitting materials for advance ruling and making deletions to satisfy Customs officials raises serious concerns about "prior restraint." In the United States, the doctrine of prior restraint prevents government from suppressing the distribution and exhibition of films, records, and other publications by the actions of police officers or other officials unless the government ensures that such action will be followed by a prompt judicial determination of whether the material is obscene. Unfortunately, Canadian courts have yet to establish a doctrine analogous to that of prior restraint, and at present, police and Customs authorities are relatively free to take drastic action, such as confiscating a dealer's entire inventory prior to any determination that the material is obscene.

f. PROVINCIAL FILM REVIEW BOARDS

Although obscenity law, being criminal law, is within the exclusive jurisdiction of the federal Parliament, the Supreme Court has held that provincial legislatures may establish film review boards and give them the power to classify and censor films. As a result, most provinces have such boards. A distributor or exhibitor of a film or video may find that a work is considered unacceptable by a local board and will be in violation of provincial law if he or she distributes or exhibits it, even to an adult audience.

It is important to note that even if a work is not obscene under the Criminal Code, a provincial board has the jurisdiction to censor it. Conversely, the fact that a film or video has been approved by a provincial board is no guarantee that the work will not be found to be obscene, or to be child pornography, under the Criminal Code.

The Ontario Court of Appeal held in the recent *R. v. Hawkins* case that the approval of a provincial board is *evidence* that the material meets the community standards test for purposes of avoiding any obscenity conviction, but it is open to the Crown to counter that evidence with other evidence showing that the material would not be tolerated by the Canadian community.

g. OBSCENITY LAW IN THE UNITED STATES

For artists who are interested in exhibiting their works in the United States, it is important to have an understanding of American obscenity law. Unlike Canadian obscenity law which, as stated above, is within the exclusive jurisdiction of the federal Parliament, in the United States obscenity is controlled locally through city ordinances, at the state level through criminal legislation, and also by federal interstate and postal laws.

Obscene material is not protected by the guarantee of freedom of speech under the first amendment of the U.S. Constitution. However, in order to be valid, U.S. obscenity laws must meet the three-part test set out by the Supreme Court of the United States in the seminal 1973 decision, *Miller v. California*. The court stated that in considering whether material is obscene, a court must ask:

   (a) whether the average person applying contemporary community standards would find that the work taken as a whole appeals to the prurient interest,

   (b) whether the work depicts or describes, in a patently offensive way, sexual conduct specifically defined by the applicable state law, and

   (c) whether the work, taken as a whole, lacks serious literary, artistic, political, or scientific value.

Community standards in the United States do not necessarily mean standards of the national community; courts have the discretion to decide what is the relevant community.

h. SUMMARY

Though there have been many attempts in legislation and judicial interpretation to clarify the confusing issues that arise in obscenity law, the basic goal of controlling obscenity without censoring legitimate art remains elusive. Some members of the community argue that art has degenerated and that, as one commentator put it, "if only sensationalism masquerading as art is at stake, we suffer no great loss if obscenity doctrine does not protect this work."

On the other hand, it may be argued that there is a dramatic clash between lay notions of art and actual artistic practice, and neither the community nor the courts should be the final arbiters of what is art and what is not. We can only imagine the works of art that may be prevented from being exhibited, or indeed from even being created, by the threat of prosecution under obscenity law.

4

ART DEALERS AND ARTISTS —
THE COMMERCIAL LINK

by Stephen B. Smart

The relationship developed between an artist and the art dealer who represents his or her work can have a tremendous influence on the direction of the careers of both of them. Many of Canada's senior artists owe much to the dealers who have helped them to achieve recognition. On the other side of the coin, the reputation of art dealers is evaluated mainly in terms of the artists they represent.

But what exactly is an art dealer? What is the nature of the art dealer's obligations to the artist and to the artist's market? In this chapter, some of the issues that arise from the art dealer's role as an intermediary between artist and public are explored. Section c., the last section of the chapter, offers a comprehensive checklist of considerations that both artist and dealer will find useful in articulating their business relationship.

a. THE ART DEALER

1. The role of the art dealer

An art dealer is a person who buys, sells, trades, or otherwise "deals" with artwork. The art dealer creates an audience for an artist's work and then markets the work within the context of that audience.

Some art dealers represent the work of just one artist, but most represent a number of different artists. A dealer may be the sole sales representative for the artist for a given geographic area, or one of many who represent the artist's work. Many dealers sell work by an artist active in an earlier century, for example, but usually only one dealer in a given area will represent the work of a living artist.

Works of art are fragile and often require a carefully monitored environment. They also need a fair amount of space to be properly stored and exhibited. For these reasons, many dealers create a gallery to house their inventory, and consequently the terms "art dealer" and "gallery owner" have become interchangeable. Some art dealers, however, do operate independent of a gallery space and may simply sell work from a travelling portfolio.

Many dealers operate from a single location, others from several locations, such as the Bau-Xi Gallery, with outlets in Vancouver and Toronto, and the Upstairs Gallery, with outlets in Edmonton and Vancouver. Members of the Professional Art Dealers' Association, which establishes guidelines and standards for commercial art dealers in Canada, frequently cooperate with fellow members to promote the work of artists to which they hold specific geographic sales rights.

2. Public agencies and artist-controlled groups

Public agencies and non-profit groups may also operate commercial art galleries or engage the services of a professional sales representative. The Canada Crafts Council and the Open Studio, for instance, both operate marketing programs which include gallery spaces and sales representatives.

Artists may also band together to organize a marketing outlet. In these cases, artists foot the bill for the operations of the gallery and hire sales assistance. Cold City Gallery, established in the mid-eighties in Toronto, is one good example of how this sort of venture can be successful. The Susan Whitney Gallery in Regina and the Wynick/Tuck Gallery in Toronto are two privately owned galleries that began as artist-controlled marketing ventures, although they have been gallery owned businesses now for a number of years.

3. How a dealer markets the work

There are two types of markets in which a dealer may be involved: the primary and secondary markets. These markets define the source from which the dealer obtains artwork. In the primary market, the dealer acquires stock directly from an artist, or controls an artist's estate. Those who are involved in the secondary market obtain artwork from a source other than the artist who created the work.

Understanding the differences between the two types of art markets is important because they demand from the dealer two very different kinds of responsibilities and obligations. In the primary market, for instance, the dealer creates demand for an artist's work by helping build his or her reputation. The regular solo exhibition of an artist's work, usually held every two years, is one cornerstone of the promotional process; the group exhibition of regular or new gallery artists is another.

For most dealers, however, marketing an artist's work goes far beyond organizing exhibitions and finding buyers. Dealers may lobby public art galleries to represent their artists in exhibitions, or propose commissioning projects and then find corporate sponsors for those projects. They may assist the artist in obtaining grants from government agencies or private institutions. They may seek unusual opportunities to raise awareness of an artist's work — convincing a magazine to use the work of an artist on the cover of an issue, for example.

A dealer may also play an influential role in an artist's creative development and how the development is received by the public. Often dealers become sounding boards for artists who are wanting to work on new ideas and may give artists valuable advice on the viability of their ideas within the context of the current market conditions. As well, many dealers exercise control over an artist's output by selecting and promoting works they feel best represent the artist's ability.

Dealers who are involved in the secondary market, on the other hand, are usually selling work by artists with well-established reputations and, therefore, they do not have to become as involved in creating demand for the work. In the secondary market, the dealer does not usually negotiate directly with an artist but instead with the current owner of the artwork.

Most dealers are involved in both primary and secondary markets. Diversifying interests helps maintain solvency, plain and simple. Also, for dealers who are the recognized sales agents for particular artists, the acceptance of works for resale ensures their hold over that artist's market.

In order to consolidate their market, however, most dealers specialize in artwork of a particular type. Galleries such as the Isaacs/Innuit Gallery (Toronto) and Fehely Fine Arts Ltd. (Toronto) are specialists in Inuit art. The Equinox Gallery (Vancouver), Sable Castelli Gallery (Toronto), and the Galerie René Blouin (Montreal) represent contemporary Canadian artists; Olga Korper Gallery (Toronto) is one of the few galleries in Canada to make a real commitment to contemporary Canadian sculpture. Some galleries, such as the Mira Godard Gallery (Toronto), have broader aesthetic focus in varying media.

The artist must be aware of the many distinctions in art dealers and must understand the specific nature of the art dealer he or she may associate with and how it may affect the market potential and success of his or her work. As Montreal gallery owner René Blouin puts it:

> When artists approach me to represent their work, I only wish they would interview me as

much as I interview them. Am I the right gallery for them? Will I be able to meet their needs? Is their work compatible with the rest of my gallery? I insist that potential artists seek references from some of my existing artists to assure themselves that my gallery is right for them. Too many artists assume my gallery suits their work without understanding what my gallery is all about. As much as I study the artist's background and career, I would hope the artist would examine the background and career history of the gallery before making a decision to commit to this important relationship. Ultimately, of course, my decision is based not only on my belief that the person is an incredible artist, but that the "chemistry" is right.

b. THE ARTIST/DEALER RELATIONSHIP

In the summer of 1990, Georgian Bay artist John Hartman found himself in a downtown Toronto courtroom in the middle of a legal dispute between two of Canada's veteran art gallery owners. The problem arose when Hartman left some of his work on a trial basis with one dealer and subsequently established an agreement with the other dealer to sell his work. Both dealers then claimed the exclusive right to represent Hartman's work, and off to court they went.

The court established that accepting artwork on a trial basis was not enough of a commitment to qualify the first art dealer as Hartman's exclusive sales representative. The negotiations held between Hartman and the second dealer, however, could be clearly documented. The court, therefore, upheld the second art dealer's claim to sales representation.

As this situation indicates, disputes over the representation of an artist can be so confused and bitter that they require legal intervention to sort out. Moreover, such disputes can have ᴀ disastrous effect on the artist. Flattering as it may have been for Hartman to have his work in such great demand, the publicity surrounding the ensuing legal battle could have damaged the reputation of everyone involved.

The key to a healthy and prosperous relationship between an artist and dealer ultimately depends upon a good understanding of each other's duties and obligations. Understanding is established with clear written or oral communication. As Toronto dealer Frank Costin says, "We keep a hands on approach in the relationship we have with our artists. Regular ongoing contact keeps issues under control. When I spot trouble I immediately get on the phone to the artist to sort out the problem." These oral communications in their own way form the contractual basis of the relationship.

The relationship between the artist and the art dealer can be looked at from three legal viewpoints. One view is that the artist provides artwork to a commercial gallery and in exchange receives from the gallery marketing services for the work. Legally, this relationship is based on that understanding or contract. Both artist and gallery are free to negotiate the terms and conditions of their business contract, and both will then be held to their bargain. Under contract law, the artist and dealer would be looked at as equals.

A second view is that when an artist places his or her artwork with the dealer, the agent will be held accountable to the artist to carry out the purpose of the business relationship. The dealer will have to account for all his or her actions as they relate to the artwork. In legal terms, this is a relationship of principal (the artist) and agent (the dealer).

A third view is that the dealer owes a *fiduciary obligation* to the artist to protect the artist's interests based on his or her position of trust. A fiduciary obligation is a device to effect justice when disputes arise. The dealer has power and control

rtwork and the artist's reputation; the artist de-
ne dealer for honest and fair dealing. This is not a
necessarily agreed upon at the start by the artist
but one that has become defined by the courts
over the years.

The complex relationship between artist and dealer may
often be a mixture of all three views: our courts might resolve
some disputes according to contract law (What does the
contract between the parties say on the issue in dispute?);
some other disputes may be resolved by resorting to the law
of agency (What was the dealer engaged to do? Has he or she
properly carried out instructions?); and still other disputes
may be resolved by resorting to the law of fiduciary obligations (Has the dealer who has the control over the subject
matter of the agreement mishandled the artwork in any way
or failed to appropriately look after the artist's interests?).

c. PURCHASE ARRANGEMENT VERSUS CONSIGNMENT

At the beginning of the artist/gallery relationship, a decision
must be made regarding the method by which the dealer will
obtain artwork from the artist. This decision involves two
choices: purchasing the artist's work outright or receiving it
on consignment.

Putting works on consignment means that the dealer
never becomes the owner of the work, but uses his or her
facilities to market or sell it. In this case, legal ownership of
the work remains with the artist and passes directly to the
purchaser once the work is sold and paid for. At no time does
the gallery legally own the work. While some galleries put
"property of the gallery until paid in full" on the sales invoice
when a work is sent out on approval to a customer, that is a
misstatement of fact unless the gallery has purchased the
work from the artist.

In the situation where the work is purchased outright, the legal relationship is straightforward: once the artist has been paid for his or her artwork and delivers the work to the dealer, the deal is done. Title to the work passes to the dealer and the dealer can do with the work what he or she wants, subject only to the subsisting rights the artist may have under the Copyright Act. The gallery owes no other duties to the artist once payment has been made for the work.

If, however, works are put on consignment with the dealer, much more significant duties and obligations arise between the parties — largely because there still remains the task of marketing the work into the hands of a third party purchaser. Until that task is complete and the third party purchaser has paid the dealer and the dealer has paid the artist, the purpose of the relationship has not been fulfilled.

Whether a gallery purchases the art outright or on consignment is a decision largely dictated by economics. The more usual route is for a gallery to take works on consignment so that it doesn't have to commit capital to the purchase. The gallery owner makes his or her profit at the same time as the artist, and the gallery will not be obligated to put out purchase capital in advance.

There are situations, however, where a gallery might find it beneficial to purchase an artist's output and take the risk or advantage of being able to resell at a higher profit margin. A few dealers have been known to pay "survival money" to some artists in exchange for the right to own the output of the artists during the period of payroll funding. Other dealers have been known to buy up a substantial amount of inventory of an artist's existing work at rock bottom prices and then market the work in their gallery at upscale gallery prices.

The late Toronto dealer, Carmen Lamana, developed a scheme with some of his artists in which 50% of their art coming through the doors of his gallery automatically became owned by him. The artist received payment for the remaining 50% interest in the work when the work was sold.

Another known arrangement is for a gallery to pay an agreed "annual income" to an artist. At year end the balance sheet between artist and dealer is tallied based on work sold by the gallery within the year. If the proceeds received from the sale of the artist's work does not reach a total equalling the annual advance, the gallery can either take works from the artist's inventory or look to the artist to meet the shortfall. If return on sales is an amount greater than the advance, the gallery then issues a payment of the difference to the artist.

The most common arrangement between a gallery and artist is for the artist to place his or her work with the gallery owner on a straight consignment basis. Sometimes an artist uses a gallery to exhibit and sell but does not arrange with the gallery to represent the work on an ongoing basis. Often galleries are prepared to take artists' work on a trial basis, especially the work of younger or unknown artists. From an artist's viewpoint, this arrangement, while not necessarily ideal, is often better than having no dealer at all.

Even in this situation, the artist is well advised to draw a short memorandum of understanding or letter of agreement. This agreement should include the following:

(a) Confirmation that the work remains the property of the artist until sold and the artist is paid

(b) Description of the financial arrangement between the artist and dealer

(c) Confirmation of who is responsible for insuring the work

(d) Acknowledgment of the artist's right to take the work back from the gallery on demand.

Similarly, when an artist has chosen a gallery to represent his or her work on an ongoing basis, the artist is well advised to put in writing the terms of the relationship with that gallery.

Other issues concerning contractual arrangements are discussed in the following section.

d. CONTRACTS

Contracts can take different shapes: detailed written contracts signed by the parties; letters of agreement where the contract is set out in correspondence between the parties; or simple verbal agreements. All are legal, but problems can arise when agreements are not clear or do not cover some point in dispute.

When oral contracts come into dispute, there is the added difficulty of proving what was said. This pits one person's version of the facts against the other's, so a judge will have to evaluate the credibility of each party.

There seems to be a general assumption in Canada that most artists have written contracts with the galleries that represent them. This is not true. A random survey undertaken of reputable galleries in Vancouver, Calgary, Toronto, and Montreal disclosed that very few galleries either have or want the relationship between gallery and artist to be "clouded" by a formal written contract. Andy Sylvester of the Equinox Gallery in Vancouver noted that, in the few cases where the gallery did have written contracts, disputes seem to have arisen. His gallery's approach is to give new artists an unsigned memorandum or letter describing the basic features of "how business is done" between the artist and the gallery.

When disputes arise and there is no written contract, however, the problem might often be resolved in favor of the person having the greater power in the relationship, rather than by what may be right or reasonable under the circumstance — more often than not this person would be the dealer. Gallery owner René Blouin states that when problems have arisen between him and the artist, he steps back, opens his books up to the artist, and gives the advantage to the artist. He says, "What's a few dollars when what we are talking about are reputations and art?" While this attitude might explain the success of his gallery, for most artists, trust is not enough to cement a business relationship. Most gallery owners, pressured by their own financial and business concerns, might not offer their artists such free access to the books and records of their galleries.

In the case of a dispute, the courts will first look at the written documentary evidence that exists to determine the respective obligations of the parties. If there is no written or documentary evidence, they will consider what the parties say were their oral contractual arrangements. And when written or oral contracts do not cover the point disputed, the courts may be compelled to imply a contractual term into the relationship to cover the point.

Even though oral contracts are legally valid, it's important to have written documentation of the relationship between an artist and the dealer, as it is such an important business relationship. A contract should spell out the terms of that relationship, who has what responsibility to complete which task, who is financially responsible for which aspect of the relationship, and how the financial sales results of the relationship are to be shared.

Without a written agreement, uncertainty can occur, which in turn can lead to a breakdown of the relationship and either costly court encounters or simply the surrender by the weaker to the stronger.

e. A CONTRACT CHECKLIST

Contracts are only as good as the time spent on creating them:

- Are the terms clear?

- Are the terms concise?

- Do the terms cover all the major points?

The following sections provide a checklist of items both the artist and the artist's representative should consider in articulating their business relationship. The issues raised point out the complexity and importance in the relationship between artist and dealer. How matters are addressed in any situation may depend on the attitude and resolve of each party in any given scenario.

The purpose of the following checklist is to raise the awareness of addressing and resolving certain issues up front before they get out of hand and lead to an unnecessary breakdown in what otherwise is a constructive and mutually beneficial relationship.

1.   What is the term or duration of the agreement?

How long do you want this important business relationship to last? One year? Five years? Forever? Address this point.

Do you want this relationship to be for your career (unless things go wrong), or do you intend it to be for a few years at which point it will be re-evaluated? Should the agreement provide that it will continue indefinitely unless terminated by either party?

2.   How does the relationship get terminated if one of the parties wants out?

This issue of termination is a companion to the issue of the duration of the contract. If the contract is for an indefinite period of time, include in your contract or letter of agreement a clause that provides the right of either party to terminate the agreement on six months' written notice to the other (or whatever time period seems reasonable to both of you). A termination clause provides an escape hatch if the relationship turns sour or if one of the parties simply wants to move on to a different opportunity.

Decide how notice is to be given. Should it be in writing? Should the notice be by registered mail? Where should notice be delivered to?

The courts recognize the legal right of parties to terminate their relationship on reasonable notice unless the contract makes it clear that the parties have agreed to a "forever" relationship. What is reasonable notice is determined by a number of factors: how long the parties have been associated with one another; to what degree either party may have invested time and money into the relationship so that the "investment" receives some recognition before peremptory cancellation; and so on.

In some cases, a 30-day notice may be appropriate and in others a six-month or one-year notice of termination may be more reasonable. Each case has to be assessed on its own facts. The penalty for premature termination of contract (i.e., failure to give reasonable time notice of termination) can result in a claim for damages from the other party.

3. Is the contract "exclusive"?

The issue of exclusivity by geographic area is important. Galleries in Canada are usually locally based in a single metropolitan area. Many gallery owners establish that they are the exclusive agents of the artist's entire output wherever sold, or at least the exclusive dealer within Canada. A successful artist may wish to have the freedom to exhibit and sell his or her works in other regions of Canada without necessarily being tied to a home town dealer.

Before signing a contract, be sure to address the following important considerations:

(a) Does the gallery have an active marketing program for gallery artists outside the metropolitan area in which it is situated?

(b) Who is better equipped to arrange representation outside the immediate geographic area of the artist or his or her gallery? Sometimes the artist is just as easily positioned to arrange shows or have commercial gallery representation outside the original metropolitan area as the gallery owner is.

(c) Is this issue one that should be addressed at a later date, once some history and experience have developed between the artist and his or her dealer? One way of approaching this issue is for the agreement to begin with the dealer being an exclusive agent limited to the geographic area within, for example, 200 kilometres of the location of the gallery. The parties could then be free to expand on that geographic area later on.

(d) Many competent and successful artists today are concerned about international representation. Accordingly, the same considerations apply as to whether the external representation should be through the domestic gallery representative or whether the artist wishes the freedom to negotiate this issue himself or herself.

4. What are the financial arrangements?

The commission rate a gallery is entitled to on the sale of artwork is of utmost importance to both parties and, therefore, to the success and comfort level of their relationship. This issue must be discussed and agreed upon in writing by the parties at the beginning of their relationship so that the rate cannot then be changed without further mutual agreement.

Commission rates vary, but are often 50% of the net sale price of the artwork. The gross sale price of an artwork is the price it sells for. Net sale price is the balance after repayment to the artist or gallery of certain costs, such as framing, production, transportation, etc. As these costs can be substantial, their treatment under a contract should be considered specifically and separately.

The artist and dealer should also agree on the gallery's commission rate if the artist's work is sold at another gallery outside the geographic area of the "home base" (usually 10% to the home gallery and 40% to the new gallery) and if a specific work is commissioned by a purchaser (usually 30%, but often varies and is the subject of specific negotiation).

Finally, the contract should address at what point the artist is to receive his or her share of the sale proceeds: On the date the sale is completed? Within 30 days of the sale (to permit a reasonable time for the purchaser to pay the dealer)? Or when the final payment is made by the purchaser? This issue has often created bad feelings between gallery and artist. It is in both their interests to address and resolve this issue up front.

5. What are the usual obligations of the artist?

The artist is usually responsible to the gallery for a number of matters which should be addressed in the contract:

(a) Completing artwork for an agreed-upon exhibition schedule

(b) Providing updated artwork to the dealer between shows as it becomes available

(c) Presenting artwork in an acceptable form for exhibition, often but not always including the framing costs of the work for exhibition purposes

(d) Insuring the work until it is sent to the gallery

(e) Providing the gallery with information regarding studio sales made outside the gallery

6. What are the usual obligations of the gallery?

Again, the gallery's obligations should be specifically addressed in the agreement. Some of the following represent ideas for discussion and may or may not be actually included in written documentation:

(a) Exhibiting the artwork responsibly and fairly and having solo exhibitions of the work within an agreed-upon exhibition schedule

(b) Promoting the work by seeing that there is appropriate advertising in local newspapers, regional, and national art journals and magazines

(c) Maintaining a current mailing list of persons potentially interested in the work and undertaking a mailing on an appropriate basis

(d) Providing the receptions at the opening of exhibitions

(e) When appropriate, seeking exposure to the work in appropriate public galleries including considering the arrangement of travelling shows

(f) Arranging and/or promoting news releases, catalogues, brochures, or other informational material as may be appropriate to the specific exhibition

(g) Assisting the artist in having grant information or other funding possibilities made available to him or her

(h) Assisting the artist in reviewing and editing what work will be shown in any particular exhibition

(i) Keeping the artist advised of all sales

(j) Assuming the cost of shipping the work to purchasers when the work is sold or is out on approval

(k) Promptly remitting the artist his or her share of the net proceeds of the sale

(l) Advising purchasers of the artist's copyright and exhibition rights and that the artist still owns legal title to the work until it has been paid for in full

(m) Using care in letting works leave the gallery on an approval basis (Does the gallery know the person taking the work on approval? For how long will the work be on approval?)

(n) Ensuring that payment arrangements with purchasers are realistic and protect the artist

(o) Keeping the artist informed on a timely and regular basis of all substantial issues relating to the artwork, sales, inventory, and status of accounts between the parties (Agree how often the gallery owner should provide a regular status report on all issues and insist on adherence to this schedule.)

7. **What obligations do the artist and the gallery share?**

(a) Establishing the price at which the work should be marketed and providing for a periodic review of the pricing of the work (This is an exceedingly important concern. Both parties must be satisfied with the establishment of price levels. There must also be a clear understanding of those circumstances under which the dealer may deviate from price levels.)

(b) Establishing the commission rate the gallery will be entitled to on the sale of work including what costs, if any, will be deducted from the gross selling price before the net proceeds are divided

(c) Agreeing on what discounts should be offered to consultants or certain special purchasers such as a corporation or another dealer purchasing outright

(d) Deciding who is responsible for the costs associated with storing the artist's inventory if it is stored outside the gallery space and working out how the dealer and artist can access the inventory in storage if necessary

5

ART AUCTIONS

by Stephen B. Smart

The spring and fall art auctions held by auction houses in Toronto, Montreal, Calgary, and Vancouver have become a traditional part of the art landscape of Canada. It is there that a substantial amount of the total art sales in Canada in any given year are transacted. It is there that the market is tested for who's hot and who's not. It is there that trends in collecting are observed. And it is there that from time to time an unsuspecting buyer, seller, or auctioneer can become embroiled in a legal snarl following the auction dance.

The auction process, while normally straightforward, can and does present pitfalls for the unwary. It is important for all parties to understand their respective positions from a legal viewpoint.

The auction house, in fact, plays a pivotal role in the art market worldwide. It provides perhaps the only venue in which the value of an artist's work is determined as much by the buyer as the seller, and that more equal relationship provides a realistic basis for pricing an artist's work. And make no mistake — the amount an artist's work sells for (or doesn't sell for) at auction will affect the pricing of that artist's work elsewhere.

a. UNDERSTANDING THE AUCTION LANDSCAPE

1. Types of auctions

The idea behind an auction is straightforward. Articles are offered for sale to the public and sold to the person who makes the highest bid. An auction differs from other retail practices, being a one-time event in which buyers, competing with other buyers, determine the value of an article.

In Canada, auctions are run on a regular basis by professional auction houses. They can be used to sell one item, such as land, or a series of items such as farm stock, machinery, jewelry, antiques and, of course, fine art. Articles may be sold individually or as part of a group. Each article or group of articles initiating bidding activity is called a lot. Lots in auctions dealing with fine art usually consist of one artwork.

From time to time, charities or non-profit groups such as theaters, art groups, symphonies, or hospitals may also organize auctions to raise funds for a particular cause or project. While these auctions often operate according to "normal" auction rules as described in this chapter, they also often use a "silent auction" and in some cases a "Dutch auction."

A silent auction is where there is no auctioneer. In the auctioneer's place is a piece of paper in front of each object offered for sale. Bidders can circulate around the room and place a bid on an artwork by writing their name and the amount they are prepared to pay for the work. If a person is prepared to pay more than the last person, he or she simply strikes off that person's name and places the higher bid. When the time period expires, the last person on the list will have bought the work for his or her stated price.

In a Dutch auction, the auctioneer starts the bidding at a high price and invites members of the audience to purchase the item at that price. If no one steps forward, the auctioneer lowers the price by an amount he or she feels is appropriate. This process continues until someone agrees to pay the price. The auctioneer offers to sell and the purchaser accepts the offer (a reverse from the normal auction practice where the purchaser offers and the auctioneer accepts). In a Dutch auction there is only one bidder: the first person to agree to pay. A person who really wants the work but hopes for a low price can be out-foxed by waiting too long as another member of the audience steps up to accept the auctioneer's price and puts that auction to an end.

2. The role of the auctioneer

The auctioneer is the person who negotiates the sale of the articles. The auctioneer is to get the best possible price on behalf of the consignor — the person who has placed articles for sale with the auctioneer. Accordingly, the auctioneer will "work the crowd" in hopes of getting the best possible price.

When the auctioneer believes the highest bid has been reached, he or she serves notice to the assembled crowd that bidding will halt. Then at the discretion of the auctioneer ("going once, going twice, ...") down comes the hammer and, bang, a sale is made.

In an auction, it is the slam of the hammer that indicates an agreement to sell and to purchase has been reached. This agreement is a contract, legally enforceable by each party.

But suppose as the hammer is falling, another person in the audience puts forward a higher offer a split second before the hammer hits the stand. What then? Who has the right to purchase the artwork? The highest bidder or the bidder whose bid the auctioneer recognized as the hammer fell? What about the person who put the work up for sale ? Does he or she lose the higher return because the auctioneer did not notice the highest bidder?

Generally, the slam of the hammer ends matters. The auctioneer, however, may retain the right to re-open the bidding process if an overlooked bid is brought to his or her attention as the hammer falls. Therefore, a slam of the hammer is not always the end of it. While a sales contract is achieved at that point, the conditions of the auction may allow the contract to be immediately re-opened. The organizers usually make auction terms available to bidders in written form, most often found in the auction catalogue.

3. Removing your bid

Suppose you, the purchaser, have made an offer to pay a certain price and you get nervous. You are desperate for another bid to come from the audience to relieve you from paying the price that in a wild frenzy you put forward. A long pause — it seems no other bids are surfacing. Can you withdraw your bid?

A bid is only an offer that, until accepted, you are free to withdraw. Remember, however, that you have to clearly communicate your withdrawal to the auctioneer before the hammer falls. If the auctioneer does not receive your message to withdraw, your offer may still be accepted.

Another problem can occur after a successful bid. You may later realize that the excitement of the moment got the better of you. As much as you like the piece of art, you simply cannot afford your new purchase. Can you return it?

Sotheby's recent catalogue deals with the issue in its terms of sale: "... on the fall of the auctioneer's hammer, title to the offered lot will pass to the highest bidder acknowledged by the auctioneer, and such bidder thereupon (a) assumes full risk and responsibility therefore, and (b) will immediately pay the full purchase price or such part as we may require."

Buying the title means you've bought the work, lock, stock, and barrel, so forget about trying to return it and begin thinking about how you're going to pay for it.

4. The purchaser's responsibilities

Auction rules generally require that the purchased goods be removed within three days of purchase. The cost of picking up the artwork and having it transported to the purchaser's destination (including any insurance costs) is the responsibility of the purchaser.

The normal practice is that the work is paid for within the three-day pick-up period. Arrangements are sometimes made to make payments over time, depending on the circumstances, but the auctioneer does need some form of security in case the purchaser's cheque does not clear and so he or she can pay the consignor the proceeds of the sale.

The auctioneer at all times has the right to compel full payment from the purchaser. In addition, however, the auctioneer's conditions of sale often stipulate that the auctioneer (and possibly the consignor) has the right to cancel the sale or to resell the work if it is not paid for. When the latter option is chosen, the purchaser may still be liable for any deficiency if the work does not maintain its price level on the second sale. Sometimes auctions provide in their conditions of sale that if the purchaser defaults on payment in any way, the auctioneer may keep possession of the work until the issue is resolved.

b. AUCTION RULES

To avoid legal liability — or just misunderstanding — it is important to understand the auction rules, some of which are simple but technical. Many of the rules of auction houses have been developed over the years by custom. Often the rules are published in the catalogue, but many times they are not. Sometimes an auctioneer will announce at the beginning of the event any applicable special rules for the specific auction, but often the auction will simply proceed by custom.

1. Who is the seller?

An auctioneer, in selling artwork, usually acts as an agent of the consignor — the seller. Sometimes, however, an auction house may sell work that it owns.

Establishing the identity of the owner of a work is important because it will indicate whether or not the auctioneer has a vested interest in selling the work for the best possible price. The identity of the owner should be listed in the catalogue. The general practice is that the work is offered for sale on consignment unless specifically noted in the catalogue.

2. Estimates of value

The catalogue usually lists a range of values for each lot. The range, which consists of a low and high value, is determined by first examining how similar works (by the same artist or school or artists, from roughly the same time period or aesthetic approach), have done in previous sales, and then adjusting these values to reflect the demands of the current economic climate.

The values are estimates. They do not establish a fixed price range. The bidder should be the ultimate judge of what is a fair price for the work offered for sale. Auction houses try to make it clear that the range of estimated values is just that — an estimate of what the work will likely sell for. Some work will sell for higher prices, many for lower, others will not even sell.

3. Reserve bids

In many cases, artwork is offered for sale subject to a reserve. A reserve is the lowest price a consignor will accept in putting the work up for auction. It is the way in which a consigner may protect his or her investment.

Usually (but not always) a reserve is a figure that is slightly below the low end of the projected estimate. The reserve is a confidential matter between the auctioneer and seller and bidders do not know what that figure is.

The actual consignor is usually not entitled to bid. But in the case of a reserve bid being placed, the auctioneer, in acting as the agent for the consignor, can bid on the work in order to keep the price rising until it reaches the reserve level. Purchasers need to be aware that in the lower end of the bidding the auctioneer may be trying to stimulate the bidding up to the seller's reserve bid. If the work does not attract bids equal to the reserve, then the piece is not sold and is "bought in" by the auction house. In this case, the work can be re-offered for sale at a future auction.

The auction house may charge the consignor for certain administrative costs even if a work doesn't sell. These costs may include a reduced commission rate to the auction house for its efforts to sell the work, costs associated with the sales catalogue, or other special costs.

If, through oversight, the work is sold by the auctioneer below the reserve price set by the consignor, the auction house will be liable to the consignor for the difference between the reserve price and the price at which the work was sold.

4. Bidding

Bidding is usually done by raising a hand or, in the more substantial auction houses, by raising a bidding paddle obtained from the registration desk. In some cases, when a bidder wants complete anonymity, he or she will arrange for another person to bid on his or her behalf. This is often done on an informal basis and, depending on the circumstances, may involve paying a fee to the person who does the bidding.

Pre-bidding may be made in writing and left with the auctioneer before the sale. Alternatively, bids may often be accepted by telephone as the auction proceeds.

It is not always the bidder who sets the bid. If an auctioneer is not satisfied with the amount by which a bid has increased, the auctioneer can refuse the bid and sell to the previous bidder.

c. THE RELATIONSHIP BETWEEN THE SELLER AND THE AUCTIONEER

There are a number of issues of mutual interest to the auctioneer and consignor. First, both will want to identify and agree that an auction is the appropriate vehicle for selling the work. Many works are best sold through the auction process, but in other cases, the seller may be well advised to market his or her artwork through a different channel.

If the work is suitable for auction, will the work appeal to the clientele of this particular auction house? Should the work be in its major seasonal auction or a more minor one? Good decision making on these issues is equally important. There is no use putting a work for auction that does not suit the clientele. The correct matching of work and specific auction market produces the best results for all parties.

Second, it is important to verify the authenticity, or "authorship," of the work. It is in the interests of auction houses to try to establish to the best of their ability the authenticity of all work in an auction in order to maintain their reputations as credible dealers. An auction house may refuse to represent work that cannot be properly documented or identified.

Sellers can aid this process by providing the most accurate data possible to verify the work. It certainly enhances the chances of having work accepted for sale by providing the proper documentation and other relevant information. Authenticity or "authorship" of a work can often be established by provenance, which is the documented history of the artwork: who has owned the work since it was created, where the work has been exhibited, what documents are available to establish the pedigree, etc.

If the auction house accepts a work for sale without the proper documentation, it may use any number of methods to establish authenticity, at no extra cost to the consignor. These methods include thoroughly examining the work, comparing it to similar works by the artist, using ultra-violet light examination and radiographs, and researching historical documents. When an auction house cannot clearly identify a work of art as being by a specific artist, it may use qualifying words such as "in the manner of Krieghoff" or "attributed to Tom Thompson" or "in the school of Verner."

A third concern is setting the suggested range of values for the sale price. A price that is too high will discourage bidding. Being realistic and understanding the given market economy is the goal. Setting a realistic reserve bid is also of concern. While getting the highest price is in the interests of both the auctioneer and consignor, setting too high a reserve accomplishes little.

Both seller and auction house should establish what costs are the seller's responsibility whether the work sells or not. What catalogue costs, if any, are payable? What commission rate is the consignor liable for if the work does or does not sell? Who is responsible for insuring the work while the work is at the auctioneer's premises? When does insurance protection commence?

The seller should also determine when he or she will be paid following the sale. It is usual to give the auctioneer 30 days from the date of sale to clear the payments from the purchaser. However, the consignor is entitled to be paid regardless of whether the auction house has collected the purchase money or not.

Finally, a wise and cautious consignor will not leave a work at the auction house premises (even for inspection or appraisal purposes) without obtaining a written receipt that fairly and accurately describes the work. The receipt should also address the amount of insurance in place while the work is under the control of the auction house.

d. THE RELATIONSHIP BETWEEN THE PURCHASER AND THE AUCTIONEER

The purchaser is often someone totally unknown to the auctioneer who merely appears on the day of the auction. The purchaser is just that — a consumer of art who appears on auction night, bids, purchases, and pays for the goods. In the relationship between the purchaser and auctioneer, the following issues are of common concern.

1. Terms and conditions of auction

As stated earlier in this chapter, the "rules" of the auction usually are written in the program notes of the sale and are dictated by the auction house. Read the rules.

2. Authenticity

The purchaser will and should be able to rely on the details regarding authenticity or authorship of the work as stated in the auction catalogue. While the purchaser is well advised to examine the work carefully beforehand, it is clear that when an auction house says a work is by a certain artist, the purchaser may rely on this material representation.

3. Provenance

Because the provenance or other representations such as the medium or vintage of the artwork can affect value, the buyer should be able to rely on the details regarding these items described in the catalogue. If the representation is inaccurate, the auctioneer, and possibly the consignor, may be liable for damages.

The written conditions of sale often attempt to protect the auction house as much as possible on these issues. Holding out information, however, is still holding out information. Damages in cases of misrepresentation might be assessed as being the difference between the price the purchaser paid and the price the work would have sold for if the misrepresentation had not been made.

4. Value of the work

When an auction house sets a range of estimated values of the work in the catalogue, it is putting its reputation on the line for its expertise in appraising work. In a sense, it is saying to the bidding public that this is approximately what the work is worth under the market conditions at the time in which the auction is to take place. The bidding public should also be aware that a particular consignor may have insisted on the work carrying a specific estimated value as a condition of being in the auction, although auction houses generally do not like this kind of arrangement.

If a purchaser pays within the estimated range and it subsequently turns out that the true market value of the work is absolutely nowhere near that value, it is unclear whether the auction house may bear some responsibility to the purchaser. The better view would be that the estimated values are just that — estimates, not guarantees, and it is the purchaser's responsibility to research the fair value.

5. Legal title

In selling a work, an auction house implies that legal title to the work will pass to the purchaser. If it turns out that this is not the case — that the consignor is not the legal owner of the work, or that a third party holds a mortgage or other security in the work — then the sales contract is broken. The purchaser may then require the auction house to refund payment.

6. Additional costs

Very often in Canada there is a 10% buyer's premium on top of the final bid for artwork (in the United States it is often 15%) in addition to any applicable provincial sales tax and the federal goods and services tax.

e. THE RELATIONSHIP BETWEEN THE SELLER AND THE PURCHASER

Due to the nature of the auction process, the identities of the seller and the purchaser are confidential and not normally known to each other, so the relationship is minimal. However, some mutual concerns exist.

(a) While the auction house may be the primary target if the authenticity of a work is challenged, the seller may also be targeted by the purchaser. Similarly, a seller may be the target if erroneous information was supplied regarding the provenance of a work which affected the price.

99

(b) A seller may be subject to being sued by a purchaser who finds he or she has purchased a work to which there is no good legal title.

(c) It is the purchaser's legal obligation to pay the auction house, not the seller, directly for the work. Because the auctioneer is the agent for the seller, it may be possible (but it is not clear) that he or she could also sue a defaulting purchaser for any unpaid balance owing on the artwork.

6

COLLECTION MANAGEMENT FOR THE PRIVATE AND CORPORATE COLLECTOR

by Mary Baxter and Eve Baxter

Art collection has long been a symbol of wealth, sophistication, and intellectual prowess. But what exactly is an art collection? What motivates people to acquire objects that seem to have little functional purpose?

A collection is the result of acquiring items that are in some way related to each other. The nature of the relationship depends on what motivates or interests the collector. Some people collect the work of a particular artist. Others make no attempt to confine their selections to a particular medium or style, but simply "collect what they like." In fact, there are really only three, often interrelated, reasons that motivate collecting: to extend knowledge, to gain pleasure, and to make an investment.

The primary purpose of most public art galleries is to collect and preserve objects from our cultural heritage for the purpose of research and extending knowledge. Arts patrons, on the other hand, tend to collect for their own enjoyment. The tradition of arts patronage is long and rich; it has involved religious institutions, private individuals and, in more recent years, corporations. Patrons have played a crucial role in the support of artists and, until recently, have been the sole economic support of artists.

Nowadays, many arts patrons combine their own enjoyment of the arts with a sense of cultural obligation. Many eventually donate works from their collections to public institutions or develop public venues to feature their collections. In Canada, the different levels of governments have produced a number of incentives such as tax breaks for donations of cultural property and public art requirements in private building developments to encourage this sense of obligation in the corporate and private sectors.

Last but not least, collecting is a form of investment. People buy art because of what it can deliver on an ongoing basis, or what it can give them in the future. For museums, the return is cultural. For the patron, art provides ongoing enjoyment, the pride and prestige of ownership and, in some cases, financial profits.

a. DEVELOPING A COLLECTION: SOME PRACTICAL CONSIDERATIONS

Developing a collection, whether it be corporate or private, relies on first establishing the objectives of the collection and determining a focus to meet those objectives. But deciding on what to collect also depends on a number of practical considerations such as budget and the availability of space, either to store or display the art.

Establishing a realistic budget can only be achieved by first exploring what is available in the marketplace and the current pricing structure for artwork. A private collector on a limited budget, for example, will probably have to consider buying less expensive works such as works on paper, or saving toward a major purchase.

The collection's objectives also have to be taken into account. For instance, many companies when faced with a move to new quarters, need a large amount of artwork to place in the new premises. Is there room in the budget to do this all at once, or should it be done over a period of time? The answers to these questions depend on how urgent the need for art is and the type of artwork the company has decided to collect.

The following questions can help determine guidelines for a collection:

(a) How is the collection going to be used? Will it enhance the surroundings? Be used as a promotional device? For research or education? Is it an investment?

(b) What kind of budget are you considering? Do you need to purchase a number of works over a short period of time or can you afford to add at a more leisurely pace?

(c) Have you already made some purchases? Is there anything that ties these purchases together and that you would like to build on?

(d) What kind of work seems most available in the current market? Is it important that works are easily available?

b. THE PRIVATE COLLECTOR

In a 1991 study of the Canadian arts consumer conducted by Decima Research and les Consultants Cultur'inc Inc., it was found that most of those who purchased art did so because they fell in love with the work. Surprisingly, the proportion of individuals who reported that they purchased art for investment purposes or for home decoration was comparatively small.

Nevertheless, the idea that art can be used as a form of investment is something that is often in the back of people's minds when they acquire art, especially those who are just starting out. We have all heard stories of paintings picked up at garage sales or flea markets for $25 which turned out to be worth millions. As encouraging as these stories sound, such events happen rarely.

Yet, as earlier stated, collecting art is a form of investment in the broadest sense of the word, because it is an ongoing financial commitment that anticipates some sort of return. As with any other investment, time, research, and a thorough investigation of what the market has to offer can help the investor choose the best possible prospects. It is not coincidental that a public museum may spend upwards of ten years in research and counting pennies before making the decision to acquire one work of art. In fact, most public galleries have made it a written policy to adopt a cautious approach to acquiring works of art. Those interested in collecting art should exercise similar care.

For instance, analyzing your motivations for collecting is extremely important because it can help you take the steps needed to develop the kind of collection you want, as well as prevent problems in the future. If you are buying for reasons other than personal enjoyment, as the collector, you may have to prepare yourself for living with something you might not like. Conversely, justifying a purchase for reasons other than what really motivated you to buy it may lead to awkward situations. How will you feel if you've fallen in love with a work and told your spouse you bought it because "it was such a good buy and one day it'll make us both a fortune, you'll see" only to discover that it depreciates in value over the years?

Taking the time and effort to learn about your chosen area of focus not only makes collecting more pleasurable, but it also helps develop high standards, leading to a fine collection that can be used in a variety of ways. Private collections are perhaps the greatest source of artwork for public museums. The collection of Inuit sculpture at the Winnipeg Art Gallery, for instance, has been assembled from private holdings and is a collection of international stature. The objects and artwork presented at the William Morris exhibition in 1993 at the Art Gallery of Ontario and the National Gallery of Canada were all drawn from private Canadian collections. The McMichael Gallery in Kleinburg was founded by a private patron and currently prominent art patrons such as Ken Thomson and

Ydessa Hendeles have established galleries to share their considerable treasures with the public.

Those collecting art with an eye on financial returns must exercise special care. The investment collection takes time to fulfill its objectives mainly because it takes a long time for an artist's work to rise in value. The value of a work depends mostly on demand, often dictated by endorsements of artistic quality or historical significance from the academic community. Consequently, work by important, influential artists such as Pablo Picasso, Claude Monet, or the Group of Seven will command high prices in auction whereas work by a contemporary, relatively unknown artist will not.

Availability of an artist's work and authenticity are other important factors to consider when collecting for investment. While the work of the late Salvador Dali has been recognized in academic circles, the sheer volume of his output, coupled with the highly publicized problems regarding the authentication of certain pieces, have made his work — especially his prints — a risky investment.

In contrast, as opportunities to acquire the work of an artist become rarer, values tend to rise. The work of Vincent Van Gogh, for example, rarely appears on the auction market. When it does, however, it commands astronomical prices.

The trick in investing in art is, therefore, figuring out if there will be a future demand for an artist's work, and if that demand will produce a value which exceeds the original purchase price. Gauging future demand is much easier with historical work than contemporary work because the investment potential of an historical work can be related to patterns already established in the marketplace. But whether collecting historical or contemporary art, one must be prepared to wait a long time to realize a profit.

Those who have managed to make a successful investment in art usually spend years acquiring work. They tend to focus in one area, such as a specific time period in Canadian painting. They will often buy a number of pieces by one artist, in order to ensure that they have acquired good examples of the artist's work, and to maximize their profit on a successful choice. Most important, those who invest in art usually rely (initially at least) on the expertise of a professional art consultant or curator to assist in the development of their collection.

Finding the right consultant can be difficult. Currently in Canada there is no official association of arts consultants to ensure certain standards of conduct within the profession. In fact, many of those who advertise themselves as consultants are really art dealers: they maintain a sales inventory or accept commissions from artists or dealers for the sale of artwork. If a consultant receives a commission for selling the work from the artist or dealer and also charges the client a fee for finding the work, the consultant is compromising his or her primary obligation to the purchasing client. Consultants who have affiliated themselves with a particular artist or dealer will undoubtedly have a vested interest, resulting in a conflict of interest.

It is strongly recommended that the collector examine the mandates of other collections in which a consultant is involved. Similar collection mandates can mean that a consultant may be put into the position of deciding who should acquire work by an artist that would be appropriate for a number of collections he or she represents.

The American Association of Art Consultants has published the following recommendations for those considering an art consultant:

(a) A consultant should not maintain an inventory of artworks and should have no economic affiliations with artists, artists' estates, foundries, or other fabricators.

(b) A consultant should not accept fees or gifts from artists, artists' estates, dealers, or fabricators.

(c) A consultant should be remunerated for his or her expertise and services only by the client and should not realize any sort of financial gain from the commissioning or purchase of a specific artist or work of art.

Establishing a clear business relationship with the consultant is not only important to the collector, but also to the consultant, who must have a good understanding of the extent of his or her authority in order to operate successfully within the art market. Points that should be addressed in an agreement include the following:

(a) The responsibilities of the consultant to the collector

(b) The responsibilities of the collector to the consultant

(c) A description of the method by which the collector pays the consultant (or acknowledgment that the consultant will receive a commission from the dealer/artist)

c. THE CORPORATE COLLECTOR

1. Why corporations collect art

Most companies buy art to enhance their working environment. Because the corporate collection is usually displayed within a working environment, it is often referred to as a "working collection." Yet for many companies, an art collection is more than a feature of its decor. Collecting is also a form of corporate sponsorship, for in purchasing art — especially by contemporary living artists — companies are giving practical support to the cultural dimensions of their communities.

Companies that collect also fulfill a valuable educational function. In Canada, roughly four percent of the entire population acquires art. This low figure is a strong indication of the extent to which the visual arts are disassociated from our day-to-day existence. By placing art within the workplace, companies offer employees and clients alike an opportunity to experience first-hand what is happening in the visual arts.

So what is it that corporations receive in return? The most apparent benefit is enhancement of the workplace. In fact, a study of corporate art collecting in Canada conducted by the Council for Business and the Arts in 1978 found that, of the corporations surveyed, a move to new quarters and the redesign of existing offices were frequently cited reasons for establishing an art collection.

As their collections grow, companies often use them to project a specific image, which in turn makes the companies more visible within a community. Collecting on a theme that might reflect or appeal to a targeted market is perhaps the most popular way of using a collection to project an image. For instance, in the seventies and eighties, the Toronto Dominion Bank placed the work of Canadian artists in its branches to project a Canadian image to its customers. The Sun Life Assurance Company of Canada, which currently features the work of artists in other countries alongside Canadian artists, uses its collection to complement its image of a Canadian-based company with good international standing.

How the art collection is put to use can play a big role in expressing a company's image. The now defunct Montreal-based Lavalin corporation made itself a household name in the Canadian cultural community during the eighties because of its dynamic policy to exhibit and tour works from its collection across the country, as well as to maintain a gallery in Montreal where exhibitions of the work of Canadian artists were regularly scheduled. During the eighties, Touche Ross Limited, a financial management and accounting firm based in Toronto, developed a purchase program in collaboration with the Art Gallery of Ontario to develop and embrace a collection of 19th century master French printmakers. National law firms such as Osler, Hoskin & Harcourt and McCarthy Tetrault have created goodwill in the visual arts community by their consistent commitment over a number of years to the acquisition of works by living Canadian artists across the country.

Corporate collections have also been used to create positive working relationships between employees. In the seventies and early eighties, for example, Shell Canada put its policy regarding the democratic treatment of employees to work by inviting employees to elect an art committee from its co-workers.

The corporate art collection, therefore, can be an important tool in establishing a corporate identity, distinguishing both visually and ideologically one company from its competitors, and heightening the corporation's presence within a community or potential market.

2. Promoting a corporate collection

Companies wanting to project a certain image or identity often seek opportunities to make the collection (and consequently their name) more visible to the public. The following are just some of the different methods companies have used to promote art collections:

(a) Reproducing works represented in the collection on Christmas cards, annual reports, and calendars

(b) Loaning artwork to museums for exhibitions

(c) Producing catalogues or brochures featuring and describing major works in the collection

(d) Creating a public space to exhibit works from the collection

(e) Assigning areas for the display of new acquisitions

(f) Providing information, seminars, videos, etc., for employees

(g) Providing tours of the collection

3. Collection administration for the corporate collector

Art collections evolve over time. Keeping track of what has already been acquired, overseeing the general condition of the works, and maintaining continuity in collection goals are tasks of equal importance to acquiring. Whether the collection be corporate or private, working, educational, or archival, the establishment of a sound administrative process is essential for realizing long-term collection goals.

Generally speaking, corporate collections, like private collections, are the result of one individual's interest, usually a senior executive officer. This individual will usually assign others to look after the day-to-day details regarding the maintenance of the collection while retaining a tight hold over what is to be bought, how the collection will be used, and how it will be distributed throughout the organization.

Establishing continuity is one of the biggest problems facing collections administered in this manner. When the officer leaves, interest in collecting either ceases or changes to reflect the new management's taste. In recent years there have been many discouraging examples of precisely this sort of situation. For over 20 years, Norcen Energy Resources Ltd. collected art under the auspices of its chairman, Edmund Bovey. Upon his retirement in the late eighties, however, the collection was more or less disbanded, and half of the holdings were gifted to public art galleries. Similarly, while the purchase of Guaranty Trust in 1987 did not mean an end to collecting (that happened when the new company, Central Guaranty Trust was purchased by the Toronto Dominion Bank in 1993), it did result in a radical change in the direction of collecting. The shift in collection focus meant that many important works from the original collection were sold, and, as a result, one of the better corporate collections of Canadian art was completely devastated.

A number of approaches have been tried in order to establish continuity in corporate collecting and to counteract the effects of one individual becoming too influential in directing a collection. By the late eighties, five companies in Canada had established curatorial departments to develop their collections and to give some protection from changes in management. Many more maintained these services on a part-time basis for the same reasons. In the long run, these attempts to institutionalize collection administration did not prove to be an adequate buffer against the vagaries of upper management. By the nineties, most of these corporate curatorial services fell victim to the recession and to the new philosophies regarding corporate culture. Changes in management, new management philosophies, and restricted spending resulted in freezing spending on acquisitions as well as on programs to promote the collections both inside and outside the corporations.

The most successful approach to establishing administration for a collection seems to be to form an art committee, usually made up of a small group of senior executives or partners who participate in the selection of artwork and develop policies regarding the collection. Membership can be by appointment, election, or some sort of mandatory, rotating scheme.

There are drawbacks to using art committees. Responses to art are extremely subjective. Consequently, the greater the number of people involved, the more difficult it is to establish a strong focus for collecting. Duties have to be clearly delineated — who helps keep the records, who is the contact person for the collection, and so on — in order to prevent confusion regarding the maintenance of the collection. Finally, there are a lot of headaches involved in trying to coordinate a number of busy people to view potential purchases, let alone to discuss necessary but uninspiring details such as insurance, cataloguing, and framing.

The individual or group responsible for the collection should address the issues of collection policy and maintenance. These issues include the following:

(a) Selection methods

(b) Focus of the collection

(c) Methods of disposing art

(d) Insurance strategies

(e) Lending, promotion, and presentation

(f) Overall maintenance (framing, conservation, etc.)

Like the investment collector, the corporate collector's needs are specialized. Moreover, while the interest and support might be abundant, often there is not the time available to do the extensive groundwork involved in building a collection. As a consequence, many corporate collectors retain the services of an art consultant or another arts professional such as a freelance curator or commercial dealer to advise on collection policy and maintenance. Art consultants can also do much of the hands-on work, such as arranging the shipping, cataloguing, and installing of artwork, implementing promotional schemes, or arranging educational resources for employees.

d. COLLECTION MAINTENANCE

The person who maintains a collection is called a curator. The curator is regarded as both an educator and an art historian. Many curators are associated with a particular collection of art, but there are just as many who act independently of an association with a particular museum or collection. Interpreting and exploring the significance of art has, in fact, become big business. Curators now spend much of their time coordinating exhibitions to present certain themes and points of view; the curator has become an invaluable "editor" or "thematic coordinator" of the visual arts.

Professionally trained curators can be hired to assist with the development and maintenance of a private or corporate collection, although these kinds of collections are rarely large enough to require their services. As well, corporate collectors in particular may find it difficult to justify the expense involved in maintaining a collection to museum standards.

Whether or not a curator is retained, certain issues regarding the maintenance of a collection have to be addressed.

Who will do the buying? Who will review what has already been acquired and develop collection policies? Who will be responsible for the maintenance of the collection? The following sections deal with some of the more important details involved in curating a collection.

1. Records management

Public museums keep a variety of records for each work of art, detailing physical information such as size, subject matter, name of artist, date of work, location of purchase, date purchased, purchase value, insurance value, present location, etc. These records are essential for insuring a collection and for maintaining and conserving individual works of art. Moreover, since the museum holds its collection in trust for the public, this information is not only of value to those curating the collection, but also for those who are interested in studying a particular work of art.

For corporate and private collectors, record-keeping is an equally important facet of maintaining a collection. Vital statistics regarding artwork, a physical description, provenance and current valuation, are imperative if it is to be insured. Claims related to damage or theft need to be substantiated, and this can only be done through careful documentation of the artwork.

With corporate collections in particular, it can be very easy to lose track of art. Office renovations, departmental moves, and employees with their own ideas regarding what should be up on the walls can wreak havoc on a collection if inventory controls are not established and enforced.

Records are also valuable educational and promotional tools. They reveal details about the artist and the art itself. Many companies make it a policy to supply interpretive information about the artist and their work when installing a new work.

The utility of records should always be measured in terms of how much time they require to maintain. In museums, there are individuals whose sole function is to maintain these records. In corporations, it is more often the case that keeping the collection records is just one low-priority item for a person with many other more pressing duties.

Keeping records begins with receiving artwork and a sales receipt. This receipt is evidence of a contract. It documents the purchase and sale of artwork. This receipt should provide a physical description of all works purchased. The details on the receipt should always be checked against the actual artwork and any discrepancies dealt with before a permanent record is created.

Each object acquired is then assigned a catalogue number (frequently referred to as an "accession number.") This number allows easy identification of the work and a point of entry for the records; it is an invaluable device for helping keep track of art, especially if the collection is large. It should be affixed to the work in an unobtrusive manner using a process that will not harm the work (a label on the backing of a framed print, for instance).

The method used to number artwork is currently not standardized. Museums generally use three components: year of acquisition, source of acquisition, and order that the acquisition was received from the source. For instance, 1982.3.6 would indicate that the work was purchased in 1982, was an item on the third sales invoice received that year, and was the sixth item listed on the invoice. Whatever system is developed, it is strongly recommended that it remain consistent.

Documentation files, in which copies of sales receipts, conservation and framing invoices, details of provenance such as loans to institutions for exhibition, as well as biographical information about the artist and interpretive information about the artist's work, are also important points of reference. A registration record, which combines vital statistics and financial information on the artwork, is perhaps the most important record to be kept. This record should contain the following categories:

(a) Catalogue number

(b) Date of purchase

(c) Source of purchase

(d) Amount of purchase

(e) Tax (where applicable)

(f) Artist

(g) Title

(h) Date

(i) Description (i.e., medium, measurements, etc.)

(j) Condition (optional)

(k) Insurance value

(l) Present location

A location record, which lists artwork by location, can be extremely important, especially for a collector who moves artwork frequently or houses it in a number of different areas. Also, maintaining a photographic record, while not imperative, is perhaps one of the most useful methods for identifying artwork. The caliber of this record — whether slides, transparencies, or snapshots are used — is not important. Some collectors may use transparencies because works from their collection are frequently reproduced. Most prefer to use clear snapshots which do the job but are not that expensive to produce.

2. Insurance

Fine art insurance policies are covered by a form of inland marine insurance usually referred to as a "floater." This type of insurance offers a broad range of coverage to its holders and is specially tailored to cover the risks of property that sees a lot of handling and changes in locations. Depending on the needs of the collector, an insurance policy can be developed to cover the art collection specifically or to include it as one of a number of elements such as office equipment or household items.

Because the insurance of fine art is so specialized, it is extremely important to find a broker with experience in this field. Only a broker with a thorough knowledge of the different ways in which art can be insured will be able to devise a policy that best suits the interests of the collector.

When deciding how to insure a collection potential, risks must be weighed against expense. Most public art galleries, for instance, do not insure for an amount equalling the value of their collection. If they did so, the insurance premiums they would pay would be extraordinarily high. Also, in the protected museum environment, risks to artwork associated with daily wear and tear are relatively low. Sections of works may be damaged, but the overall chance of theft or the destruction of an entire art collection is slim to non-existent.

Since private and corporate collectors usually exercise a great amount of care in the handling of artwork, they need only choose an amount of insurance to cover the most valuable works in their collections. For corporate collectors in particular, it does not make much sense to cover low-value works (usually under $2 000) that they anticipate replacing in a few years. Also, insurance policies require documentation regarding the works, their movements, and locations. Making a clear division between what is to be insured and what is not can, therefore, have a direct effect on the amount of time spent on administering a collection. (It is not recommended, however, to completely neglect uninsured works because eventually their significance, and consequently their value, may increase to the point where they will need to be included on an insurance listing.) It is also important to remember that coverage can be extended to cover frames or other devices used to display or protect the works.

Insurance policies should cover art when it is in transit, stored at a location other than that owned by the insurer, and while loaned to another individual or institution. Establishing coverage for artwork in transit is crucial. While shipping companies — including companies specializing in the transportation and storage of fine art — must carry their own insurance, their contract with the client waives responsibility for insuring a work to its full value unless specifically requested by the client to do so. The same waiver usually applies to any individual or company such as a professional installer or conservator who has been engaged to handle the artwork.

Arrangements to loan artwork to a public institution always require some negotiation regarding insurance. In borrowing a work of art, a gallery usually undertakes responsibility for the work, including insurance, while it is on the gallery's premises, or other locations or transportation it initiates. But whose insurance covers the work when it is being transported to or from the owner? Does your insurance company need to be notified if the work will be covered by the gallery's insurance? What responsibilities the gallery will undertake and whether or not these are acceptable to your insurance company must be established before the work goes out on loan.

Insurance policies can offer full or partial compensation for damages to artwork, depending on the circumstances. A policy may cover costs of restoration or replacing the work, for instance — and, in particular, on the fair market value of the work.

Fair market value is the projected value of a work during current market conditions. It is determined by an appraiser by looking at the pricing structure of similar works (same artist at the same period of development, for instance). It can be the original purchase price if the work has been purchased recently and there has been no change in the pricing structures for that artist's work.

Insurance companies require that the appraiser be disinterested — someone who does not have a vested interest in the collection. The administrator of the collection, for instance, should not provide fair market values for the work. Many collectors rely on the Professional Art Dealers' Association for appraising work. Art experts, such as consultants, reputable art dealers, or auction houses may provide these services as well. Most appraisers charge a percentage of the total value of the work appraised (anywhere from one to two percent).

Any payment an insurance company issues on a claim is based on the fair market value of a work. For work that is lost, a full reimbursement can be made; for work that has been damaged, funds may be released for repair; if the value of the work has been affected by damage, then the work may be auctioned and the insurance company will reimburse any difference between the sale price and the amount for which the work was sold.

An insurance policy should cover all risks of loss or damage to the art. There are many, often surprising, exceptions to what a policy will cover: nuclear war; wear, tear, and gradual deterioration; damage by insects, moths, or other animal pets (this includes your household pet); inherent vice (e.g., faulty construction or use of poor materials by the artist); loss or damage resulting from repair, restoration, or retouching; breakage of fragile articles (this exception is perhaps the most surprising and is extremely out of date); mysterious disappearance or loss disclosed by taking inventory; and employee infidelity (e.g., an employee damaging a work).

What will or will not be covered varies from policy to policy. Some exclusions can be removed at no extra cost;

others can be covered through an arrangement of additional premiums, which can be expensive. It is best to begin with a policy that covers the areas of most concern for the collector. Policies that do not cover "mysterious disappearance or loss disclosed by taking inventory," or "employee infidelity," may not be particularly useful to the corporate collector. Policies that do not cover the breakage of fragile articles are no good to anyone wishing to insure fine art. These kinds of restrictions clearly indicate the importance of finding a broker who understands the collector's needs.

3. Conservation

Preventative maintenance is the best way to conserve works of art. This involves providing works with adequate protection from environmental or other hazards. For instance, measures should be taken to ensure that artwork is handled in a safe manner and any damage should be repaired promptly to safeguard it from further deterioration. Delicate works, such as works on paper, should be framed properly.

There are a number of excellent manuals regarding the proper handling techniques for art that can be recommended by your local public gallery. If more than one individual is handling the art, care should also be taken to provide written instructions on handling techniques.

The collector should not undertake the repair of artwork without proper training. Fine art restorers spend many years learning how different materials might interact, and without this specific knowledge the collector could easily risk greater damage to the work.

4. Disposing of art

Some of the reasons why people dispose of art are because they get tired of it, they want to generate capital, the work no longer fits the collection criteria, or the piece has deteriorated beyond repair.

Deciding to dispose of a work of art often takes as much questioning and soul searching as it does to buy it. Why do you have to do it? What alternatives are open to you?

How you dispose of art generally depends on why you want to dispose of it. For instance, if you wish to free up funds or cull your collection, you may decide to sell the work. Artwork can be sold through auction or an art dealer. If you choose to sell it through an art dealer, you should contact one who represents the artist's work or trades in similar work.

Another alternative is to gift artwork. Donations to public institutions do provide certain tax benefits (see chapter 7), but they have to go through an approval process. Public galleries usually have acquisition committees that reviews artwork made available to them. If you are arranging to donate artwork to a public art gallery, you should receive from them written acknowledgment of your intention and a description of the kind of assessment process used to evaluate the appropriateness of your gift.

Artwork can be donated to other public institutions such as hospitals, social services agencies, or public libraries. Gifting to these kinds of public institutions sometimes provide limited tax benefits. Artwork given to charitable auctions may also provide some tax benefits.

Work that has fulfilled its function and is no longer needed can also be returned to the artist. Many artists will accept returns of artwork, which they may resell or, as is more often the case, keep for their personal archives.

The final alternative is to destroy the work. This is a drastic measure and should only be considered if the artwork has deteriorated beyond repair. The artist's permission should be obtained before taking this step.

7

PUBLIC ART GALLERIES IN CANADA

*A conversation with Jeffrey Spalding
and Stephen B. Smart*

In recent years, there have been severe cutbacks in the government funding of Canadian public museums and galleries. In 1992, the Art Gallery of Ontario was forced to close its doors to the public for seven months and lay off a large portion of its staff. In 1993, the Art Gallery of Windsor made the radical decision to allow its premises to be used as a gambling casino and move operations elsewhere in order to raise funds.

These are perhaps the most dramatic and publicized indications of the funding crisis affecting our public art museums and galleries, but other examples are present in the day-to-day operations of every institution across the country. Fewer travelling exhibitions, longer times for showing exhibitions, shorter hours, and lay-offs are just some of the ways in which art institutions are trying to tighten their belts.

In the following interview, Jeffrey Spalding, Director of the University of Lethbridge Art Gallery, offers suggestions on how a community can get around these problems and organize a venue for exhibiting and collecting art.

*   *   *   *   *

SS: To start, give us a little bit of background on the history of public galleries in Canada. How long have they been with us in Canada?

JS: The National Gallery of Canada was founded in 1880, and the Art Gallery of Toronto, currently the

Art Gallery of Ontario, was established in 1913. For the most part, however, the public galleries in Canada are a recent phenomenon. A large percentage of galleries have turned out to be either built, founded, renovated, or expanded since our centennial year of 1967.

SS: How are galleries funded?

JS: Galleries are funded by a multi-tier system. Some are funded by the local authority, whether that might be a municipality such as a town or city, or an institution, like a university. Then there are provincial opportunities for funding from which you can get program or special project assistance or other kinds of block funding for operating. There are opportunities for federal funding as well. But funding varies from province to province and depends on the institution type.

There are two basic art museum types. One is a public gallery which has a charter under the Museums Act and is funded primarily through the public sector. The second type is an institutional gallery which, by and large, are galleries that are a part of another institution such as a college or university.

For example, the Nickel Arts Museum of the University of Calgary is an institutional gallery because its principal function presumably is to serve the needs of the institution as a teaching resource. Providing services to a wider constituency is a secondary function. Another type of institutional gallery is a corporate gallery, such as the Toronto Dominion Bank's gallery of Inuit art in Toronto.

SS: What is a public gallery really?

JS: Public galleries are set up so that they can serve any number of functions. First and foremost, there are distinctions between a public gallery and a public museum or a public art museum.

The majority of institutions that have opened up in Canada since the late 1960s have been functioning as exhibition centres. Their opportunities for collecting are almost none or restricted. Generally speaking, those galleries think that the service they provide is primarily to bring, present, or organize exhibitions. A public art museum takes on quite a different function.

Exhibition centres are unencumbered by the need to care for a collection and they don't have to bear those costs. Therefore, they can keep their resources pointed in the direction of contemporary current programming and currently identified needs.

SS: One often hears the term "parallel gallery." Is that the same as an exhibition gallery?

JS: It is presumed that parallel galleries (they don't use that phrase much any longer) are artist-run centres. The institution is run by and on behalf of artists. Artists themselves can have a direct control over what they show and, therefore, be able to enter into exhibitions of a more experimental nature without the need for curatorial authorization or intervention.

SS: Does the artist-run centre rely on public funding?

JS: Absolutely. And not just financially. Most artist-run centres rely on a good chunk of volunteer labor to start up and continue running.

SS: How does a small community get a gallery established?

JS: It depends on what they want. Classically, galleries have attached themselves to third-level educational institutions, but it doesn't have to be this kind of institution. A gallery can be attached to a high school for instance or to a hospital.

SS: Is the idea to establish links to an institution for funding reasons or just to add legitimacy to the gallery?

JS: Any combination. Some of the reasons are pragmatic; some are philosophical. Again, it depends on why the gallery is created. Institutional galleries often are established to meet specific requirements of their funding institutions — to provide exhibition space, programming, and educational facilities for performances if it is a performance centre, or artworks if it is a visual art centre. But the first order of business is what do you want out of it. Are you looking for an opportunity to showcase local or emerging regional talent, or to encourage or foster the development of regional or local talent? Or do you want to connect with something else?

Combinations with local libraries seem to work. You also can do a lot with borrowed facilities and volunteer labor. You are really looking for resources to run an exhibition program from your own community and you need to develop a support and consensus from that community.

It is when you go outside the community and require assistance — cooperation and loans from artists or institutions outside of your local group — that you have to begin to be able to provide both staffing and facilities that are more commonly standardized and accepted as professionally acceptable to care for and safeguard works of art. That's where it all starts to bump up and change.

SS: And that's where a lot of the funding is tied in to what facilities you can provide in terms of curatorial care.

JS: Yes, staffing, levels of security, environmental control, and just straightforward professional administration.

SS: Suppose there is a small community, let's say Midland, Ontario, and to date it has had only a modest art program associated with its local museum. How could it develop a "real art gallery"?

JS: Again, you have to determine what it is that you are trying to get done. What is your market? What is your potential? Do you want to provide a service exclusively for the everyday residents of your community, or do you intend to draw people from all across the region or province?

SS: The vision of what a new gallery will be affects where its creators may head for funding. In other words, if it is intended to serve a local or regional area, they ought to first head toward their municipal council or regional government.

JS: Absolutely, and of course it is not a very Canadian thing to do but you could always go to private individuals and establish a foundation. That has not been a common route although I think it is going to be increasingly the only reasonable one.

Institutional galleries are also beginning to question their purpose. Asking questions like, "Why are we in the art museum business? Why are we spending our available funds in this way?" These questions should be asked in good times as well as in bad. Bad times of course force institutions to ask these questions for pragmatic reasons.

For most small institutions, like one that might be set up in a town like Midland, the questions are these: What are its prospects? How does it provide any service? How does it develop services to deliver to its potential market? Those are really the issues. How do you get access to the art to provide to the hypothetical market or audience you are attempting to reach?

125

Most smaller institutions have neither a collection, nor much money. They often don't have first-class facilities and often they lack expertise in their staff. What that often means is that small institutions in smaller places with smaller budgets have smaller opportunities available to their community. They do the best they can with the means they have. The audiences have to learn to accept that is what they will get. That is okay and that is fair. What else can you expect of an institution that is so encumbered with those problems?

But in Lethbridge [at the University of Lethbridge Art Gallery], we decided to turn things around. We have tried to establish some kind of credibility by acquiring a collection and becoming a collection-centred institution. In establishing credibility we establish more interest, support, and funding.

SS: Could you expand on the definition of your concept of "collection-centered institution?"

JS: The larger collection-centered institutions are obvious. The majority of their floor space, budget, and staff resources are placed at the service of building collections and providing service through their collections. So when you go to the National Gallery for instance, you are primarily coming in contact with art services and art experiences provided by their permanent collection.

Community galleries, or those that serve a regional or municipal audience, were also originally established to house collections. Many of these institutions, however, have come to regard themselves as an exhibition-type centre or a centre for arts education. They put all of their effort, money, and heart into the temporary programs.

As a result, for the ten exhibitions they might hold in a year, eight would consist of temporary travelling exhibitions. Then, usually in the summer, they show whatever they might have in the vaults as filler. That is how people often get to think poorly about collections and the way in which they are exhibited. If those who run the galleries won't treat their collections seriously, neither will their audience.

SS: I understand that the bulk of the Lethbridge collection comes by way of donations from collectors?

JS: That is correct. Ninety-eight percent of the material is acquired from donations. They come from all across the nation. The majority of our donations come from outside of Alberta.

SS: When we talk about donations, very often we are thinking of collectors as principle donors. Are artists big donors too?

JS: Yes. Any individual or group who has access to materials can become a donor — an artist, an art dealer, an art collector, a corporation, or another institution, for instance.

SS: Apart from artwork itself, is it a growing concern for an art gallery to gather archival material or bibliographical materials on artists or collectors?

JS: I hope it is. Certainly it is for the larger institutions such as the National Gallery of Canada, the Public Archives of Canada, the Montreal Museum, and the Vancouver Art Gallery. These larger institutions have formidable historical archives. Clearly that is something that is really important to have available.

Tax advantages regarding the donation of this kind of material helps enormously. When there is so little money around to acquire art, however, people are going to be very reluctant to try to find money for things that are of only scholarly interest. So it is something that has grown and continues to grow because of the tax benefits associated with donations.

SS: How do you deal with the issue of quality of proposed work being donated?

JS: Well there are a lot of ways. One consideration has to do with the type of institution receiving donations. Are smaller community galleries going to start wondering whether an offered donation of a particular Picasso print is good enough for the collection? Whether it is exactly the Picasso needed? Better to ask questions such as "Does anyone in the region have one?" "Are there people in the region that would benefit from seeing it?" "Would there be some legitimate use for the object there?"

[But] you have to use different criteria depending on what institution is involved. For instance, at the University Art Gallery, we have different sets of needs. One need is for display. Another is for special study. Yet another is based on the fact that we have massive buildings. Massive buildings can be awfully empty and dull — horrible environments to be in. So there is the need for "beautification," a very important function of art. Now I would not want to be taking a work of art that is of extraordinary national significance and importance and leaving it in unsupervised surroundings. So some modest humble objects that are quite handsome may be of some value in that capacity. This kind of work helps us fulfill an obligation to the institution without diminishing the resources of our collections.

I find that many of the smaller collecting institutions are very concerned about making judgments at the point of acquisition. I prefer to take a much more open attitude than what pragmatics allow. I know that you have to keep your resources targeted at what you need to get done and that storage space can be at a premium. But for the most part, most institutions never reach the level of being fully taxed on their resources.

Moreover, tastes and reasons for being interested in art continually change and evolve. How many times have people held the view that a proposed donation was not of great value only later to find out that their judgments were incorrect?

I look for legitimate professional indicators about the artist. Is the artist a known contributor to the discipline? Can we tell through the artist's educational background, the exhibition history, the publication history, and other things if he or she is a legitimate contributor? If the answers are yes, then there may be little reason to worry. If it is a new artist, or someone who is not proven, you might have more to worry about. Those are not the kind of gifts that are ever offered anyway.

People get overly concerned about undue influence upon the public process or the public service when someone comes along with a huge gift. They feel that those sort of gifts redirect the whole institution. My view is simply that it is only one gift. There is nothing to prevent you from taking a countervailing gift, you know, that will push you into another direction. So it need not define the institution; it just may enhance the institution.

SS: A lot of people are not familiar with different institutions and so on. How would they learn what might be an appropriate place for them to donate work?

JS: It depends on what they would like to see done. For instance if you are a collector who lives in Midland, Ontario and have a work that you would like to consider for a donation — you are going to get the same tax benefit wherever it goes, you know — your criterion might simply be "I don't care, I have to donate this thing: I don't feel like selling it."

One important consideration might be who wants it. To answer that you can write or phone around to any of the institutions that you believe will be convenient to you and may be interested. If you don't know who's out there, you may be able to get a further referral from the professional you already contacted.

Another alternative is to contact the artist or the art dealer from whom you bought the work. The artist and the art dealer are in touch with these kinds of matters and either would be a good start. Or you can try to find an institution that has already expressed interest and competence in the area in which you are considering donating.

You could also try to stir enthusiasm in an institution — convince them of the importance of your gift. For instance, in 1982, the University of Lethbridge received an offer of a gift of contemporary British art. We did not have any contemporary British art but it seemed to us that since we had contemporary Canadian and American works in our collection, the British works would complement what we already were trying to do. That person had such an extraordinary interest and passion for British art that it got an institution — not just the individuals but an institution — very much excited about the idea of British contemporary art within an international framework. We have now become avid collectors of British art as a result of that initial bequest.

SS: What are the criteria for artists wishing to donate work to an institution?

JS: Subject to the work being certified under the cultural property legislation, the artist gets the same tax benefit as any other donor. An artist also has the same issues of identifying an institution which will be interested in accepting his or her work. For an artist, the same test applies: Is the work of national significance? Assuming an artist's work meets that test, then an artist can target those institutions where he or she would like the work to be. This can help establish a reputation and create a wider audience for that artist's work.

Artists also may believe that it is valuable to place their work in proximity to the work of another artist within a particular collection. For instance, someone may think that Jack Bush's painting *Dazzle Red* was personally very important and, therefore, offer his or her own work as a gift to the Art Gallery of Ontario, which owns Bush's painting. In this way the artist's own work may have the opportunity at some point in its life to be exhibited as a point of comparison with Bush's work.

Often artists feel that a work made in one place has special pertinence to that place, and should be offered to the gallery serving that particular location. Other strategic reasons for artists include trying to find institutions that are showing great promise, or are doing a lot of things with their collection. With these sorts of institutions artists can be reassured that their work will be used instead of simply being relegated to the vault.

SS: I hate to say it, but as a lawyer this conversation has given me the idea that maybe some donors who hold personal biases can compel curators to accept a proposed gift as opposed to using an objective criterion of what is in the national interest.

JS: You do not get swamped with junk when you are more accommodating. You are not taxed beyond your limits

131

to just accommodate things you would not have chosen yourself. The process of understanding, exhibiting, exploring, researching, and studying about art is a function and service of the public institutions. Galleries provide a service and that active inquisitiveness and excitement and enthusiasm for art belongs to all people. Institutions ought to be facilitators of art, not the custodians of it. The museum is not the personification of the tastes and decisions of its handful of professional staff. Instead it should try as best as possible to reflect the considered views, interests, concerns, inquisitiveness, and curiosities of the people of the time.

SS: Any other thoughts on galleries or collectors?

JS: Collectors are intellectual capital and collections create loyalties in groups of people who are interested in certain topics, as well as artists who are interested in certain topics. It is a very important contingency for a gallery to both serve and foster good relations with both artists and collectors. I am entirely convinced that developing collections continues to be a major area of development for art galleries and art museums in Canada, and one that is entirely underestimated or overshadowed by the kind of Canada Council form of programming. The days of public funding for a gallery's programming and special projects, however, is over. The country just can't afford it. So more and more institutions will invariably end up having to revert to creative methods of creating collections.

8

PUBLIC ART:
THE GOOD, THE BAD,
AND THE COMPLICATED

by Eve Baxter and Stephen B. Smart

The public's perception of art in public places is at best celebratory, often merely tolerant, and at worst confused or distressed. A lot of this ambivalence stems from the feeling that public art is yet another example of how a small elite uses its power and money to create surroundings which suit its own taste and preferences. As Harriet Senie and Sally Webster say in their book, *Critical Issues in Public Art*, "... with its built-in social focus [it] would seem to be an ideal genre for a democracy. Yet, since its inception, issues surrounding its appropriate form and placement, as well as its funding, have made public art an object of controversy more often than consensus or celebration."

In many ways, the point of view that public art is a vehicle of the elite is valid. All you need to do is look at the history books for proof. Art has traditionally been used to commemorate the activities of those in power, such as Napoleon commissioning the Arc de Triomphe, or to glorify institutions, as in Michelangelo's Sistine Chapel, or to endorse a certain perception of a nation or community's identity.

In historical terms, public art had a specific meaning. It was an expression of power — usually political or religious — that most often took the form of a monument located in a place where people could freely view it. Today the notion of public art has broadened considerably, but still retains that

133

same essence — an object to which the public has unrestrained access.

a. WHAT IS PUBLIC ART?

The term "public art" can refer to the location of a work of art, the way in which the work was funded, or the audience to which the work is directed. Sometimes it refers to all three of these factors. For instance, public agencies or governments may commission or collect art for their offices, and although the art is not always accessible to the general public, it is called "public art." At other times private corporations or individuals may commission a work of art to be located in a prominent area — the entrance to a building, for example — and these works are also called public art.

The phrase used in this chapter, "art in public places," covers any contribution made by artists toward achieving the commissioner's objectives which is intended to be accessible to the general public. A public place may be any location to which the general public has physical and/or visual access on a continual basis. This location may be publicly or privately owned; it may be an interior or exterior environment.

Art in public places is created by artists and includes all building- or landscape-related works of art. The art may be an integral feature of the building or development, such as a mural or architectural feature, or it may be independent of the development such as a free-standing sculpture. It may be located on a permanent or temporary basis.

The artwork can be created from a wide range of media by a variety of "public artists." Those might include sculptors, painters, land artists, architects, landscape architects, designers, craft workers, etc. From time to time, individuals working within the arts but not usually associated with public art (poets, authors, songwriters, and photographers, for example), have also been engaged to work on public art projects.

b. HOW ART IN PUBLIC PLACES IS COMMISSIONED

Public art is most frequently commissioned by a public agency, such as a municipal, provincial, or federal government. Most of these agencies commission art as part of their cultural programming and assign professionals to coordinate the commissioning process. Usually, the process begins with a competition from which an artist is selected to create a work.

To promote art in public spaces, a number of municipalities in Canada now require developers to sponsor commissions as part of any rezoning agreement. This initiative, often referred to as a "percent for art program," is usually supervised by a public art commission comprised of representatives from the arts community and other special interest groups. The commission guides the developer through its requirements and ensures that a fair commissioning process is observed.

Those wishing to commission work for a location that is already developed do not have to seek the approval of a public art commission. Approval from the proper departments may need to be obtained, however, if adjustments to the space are required to accommodate the artwork.

Developing a commissioned work of art is a complex process. There are a number of professional areas that public art touches on such as architecture, landscape, design, interior design, the law, administration, politics, and art history. In many cases, negotiation with government agencies and developers is required. For these reasons, anyone wishing to commission art in a public place should engage a reputable arts administrator with expertise in this area.

c. THE ARTIST AND THE ART: CONTRACT CONSIDERATIONS

1. The importance of having a contract

One of the most remarkable art stories emanating from the United States in the eighties was Richard Serra's famous public art installation entitled *Tilted Arc*, which was created, commissioned, and installed with great anticipation in Manhattan's Federal Plaza in 1981. Richard Serra is one of America's leading edge sculptors of his generation. *Tilted Arc* was the winning proposal of a significant competition, which had involved municipal planners, art consultants, art juries composed of experts, and a public art commission in its planning and administration. In terms of process and product, this public art project showed all the signs of being immensely successful. Nevertheless, once installed the public reaction was overwhelmingly negative. A certain group of people simply did not want "their open space" to be occupied by tons of steel that interfered with well worn pathways across the plaza. So vociferous was the outcry, that by 1989 city officials quietly ordered welders and construction workers to head out to the plaza after the city had darkened to torch apart the work and remove it completely from the site.

The Serra case raises a number of perplexing questions: Once created and installed, who has the right to remove a work that was created for a specific site? Who, if anyone, has the right to destroy a work of art? What remedies, if any, does the artist have to see that the integrity of his or her creation is not interfered with? How long, if at all, can an artist insist that a work stay on a site for which it was specifically created?

The need to establish the responsibilities of the artist toward the individual, company, or public agency commissioning him or her, and the need to set this agreement in writing cannot be overlooked. Public art often involves substantial costs. It can attract a lot of problems in its creation and may require special care once it is in place. A contract provides both the artist and the commissioning agent the opportunity to address these issues and any other problems that might arise in the future.

136

Keep in mind that a contract for a public art commission is quite different from one for the purchase of an already existing work. At the time of the contract, the work is only an idea; a contract may be negotiated based on, for example, a small maquette with some sketch drawings where the idea is still in very much an embryonic stage of development.

2. The parties

One of the first issues to deal with is establishing the parties to the contract. It sounds simple enough. You know the artist is one of the parties, but who is the artist dealing with?

Very often, public art is created when a downtown piece of real estate is being redeveloped, so the developer is that other person. Once the project has been completed, the project is either sold to a new owner or the project is simply turned over to its true owner for whom the developer had built this project.

The artist should, therefore, attempt to ensure that the contract is binding not only on the developer but on whomever the developer may assign or transfer the contract to in the future. It is in the artist's interest to make sure that the new or subsequent owner is bound by the terms that were agreed to by the developer. This is not always simple and sometimes it's impossible. However, the artist should endeavor to include a term in the contract that requires the developer or first owner of the project not to exit the scene without first having the next owner of the development contractually committed to the same terms and obligations as had been previously agreed on. Otherwise the artist may have little protection against any new or subsequent owner of the project.

The sculpture of Bernie Miller installed in the public park area of Toronto's new Metro Hall provides an example of how this issue can take place. In this case, Marathon Realty entered into a joint venture agreement to develop the entire project not only for its own lands but for that part of the project owned by the Municipality of Metropolitan Toronto. Miller's sculpture installation was negotiated and developed between the artist and Marathon and was located on land that ultimately was to be leased by the Municipality from Marathon. Once the whole project was complete, Marathon turned ownership of its interest in the sculpture over to the municipal government. In this instance, the artist agreed that the developer could assign its interest in the contract to the municipal government and upon transfer the developer would be relieved of any liability under the contract, and the new owner, by way of an assignment agreement, assumed obligations of the sculpture.

3. Payment

One of the primary reasons for having a written contract is to determine how and when the artist will be paid. Because public art contracts often involve substantial sums of money, the developer is not prepared to pay over the entire contract price up front. The developer needs to know that as it advances money, the artist is meeting his or her responsibilities not only in producing the work on time, but also in creating the work described and agreed to in the contract.

On the other hand, public art is usually much more complicated from the artist's viewpoint than putting paint on canvas. Typically, the artist may be consulting not only with the architects of the project but also with engineering and other technical consultants to meet the technical needs for the proper construction of the artwork. In many cases, much of the artwork may be contracted out to third-party fabricators because of the materials being used. Accordingly, the artist simply cannot fund the project without receiving much needed infusions of capital from time to time to meet construction deadlines and payroll needs.

To accommodate both parties, it is common in such contracts to develop a payment schedule over the construction phase of the artwork so that certain percentages of the total contract price are paid as certain milestones are passed. Two common payment models that might be incorporated into a contract are payments over time and payments tied to specific events. In the first case, a percentage of the total is paid when the contract is signed, after a certain period of time (perhaps four months), after another period of time, and then when the work is completed and installed to everyone's satisfaction.

When payments are tied to specific events, a portion is paid when the contract is signed, another portion on completion and acceptance of detailed drawings by the developer or owner, another portion when, in the reasonable opinion of the developer or owner of the project, the work is at least 50% fabricated, and the balance upon completion of the satisfactory installation of the work.

Both these methods of payments work. The object is to tailor the payment schedule to the needs of the particular project. When payment is tied to a schedule related to the stage of construction of the work, the parties often agree that the project administrator should be the arbiter who determines whether the artist has met his or her construction milestone and who authorizes the developer to make the next installment payment to the artist.

It is important for artists to bear in mind that all provinces have legislation that requires owners and developers by law to withhold a certain percentage of any payment advanced for a certain period of time — around 30 days — to protect unpaid workers. (In most provinces, the legislation is called the Builders' Lien Act or the Construction Lien Act. There are variations between the provinces on the percentage and time period for withholding. Check with your provincial authorities.) Once the time period has expired and no construction liens have been registered against the property by any unpaid workers, the amount withheld can and will be advanced. Artists should be aware of these provisions and contracts should address this issue.

4. Timeliness

Public art projects are very often part of the overall construction phase of a downtown real estate development plan, and artists should be aware that developers and owners will hold them to a strict timetable for construction and installation of the contracted artwork. The public art program is one small aspect of the total development. Contracts may include terms for financial penalties if deadlines are not met unless the failure to meet the deadline is totally beyond the reasonable control of the artist. Typically, the City of Toronto will not issue an occupancy permit to the developer or owner for the project unless all terms of the public art program have been complied with. In other words, an artist can hold up an entire downtown project for occupancy of a skyscraper by failing to meet deadlines.

Contracts, therefore, usually contain clauses that clearly spell out that "time is of the essence" and then go on to describe the steps a developer may take if an artist is late. This issue is often a very difficult one and a cause of much frustration. Many artists simply do not have the experience or knowledge to understand the intricacies of contracting a major public artwork and to march to the beat of the developer's scheduling drum.

When putting forward a public art proposal, artists should be sure they have the technical skills required, and that the work can be constructed within the available time frame. If necessary, the artist should seek appropriate professional advice before committing to what can be substantial construction timetables.

On the other hand, delays can just as easily be the fault of the developer due to strikes, lockouts, shortages of supplies, inefficient planning, or reasons totally beyond anyone's control. While such delays will give the artist more breathing space (and the contract should provide that delays caused by developer should expand the time available to the artist by a similar time period), the contract should also protect the artist's right to compensation if such delays are caused by the developer.

5. Copyright

Both artist and developer/owner need to seriously consider the issue of copyright when negotiating a contract for a work of public art. Unless specifically transferred by the artist to the developer/owner, copyright subsists with the artist, and this can have important implications when a public art project brings attention to a commercial development.

Think of Henry Moore's "The Archer" in front of Toronto's City Hall, or Spanish architect Calatrava's knockout steel canopy at Toronto's BCE place. Both of these works have such command of space that they become one of the major identifiers to the locations. Owners can receive much publicity from the artwork and, as a consequence, may wish to advertise or promote the work on promotional or informational material. The artwork becomes a visual tool to give special identity to the building.

Under the laws of copyright, the owner or developer must acquire the consent of the artist before using photographic reproductions of the artwork (except in the case of sculptures, which are exempt from this requirement as discussed in chapter 2, section **b.2.**). Artists generally insist on keeping copyright but are usually quite willing to grant developers limited reproduction rights regarding the work. A limited grant of copyright to the owner/developer may well be to the artist's advantage and increase his or her profile.

A contract may also contain a covenant and warranty by the artist that the proposed artwork is not in breach of any other artist's copyright. No developer wants to find out later that the proposal for which he or she has paid good money was someone else's idea and subsequently be faced with a lawsuit from another artist.

A developer may also demand a clause in the contract that the artist will not create a copy of the work or one so similar to the one being commissioned in any other public site or at least within a defined geographic territory. This ensures that the developer will have commissioned a work that is unique to the development, which is the whole point of the commissioning process.

6. The site

Public art takes many forms. It may be a sculpture, it may be stained glass over the entrance to a building, or a colored mosaic floor in the lobby floor of a downtown building, or it may be a park design including outdoor seats. At Toronto's Skydome, we see Michael Snow's fiberglass "gargoyles" incorporated into the fabric of the building, as well as a rotating display of hanging banners displayed around the exterior of the Skydome by different artists.

In many cases, a work is commissioned for a specific location in a specific public part of a building project. Very often the selection of the work is based on some form of competition for how best to deal with that very specific public space. In fact, jury competition rules require finalists to address a very clearly defined site within the development so that the jury can select the proposal that, in their opinion, best deals with the particular site.

Once installed, how long must the developer/owner keep the work in that particular location or on the site at all? Is the owner free to move the work? Suppose a tiled floor was installed in the lobby of a building. Can the owner subdivide the lobby area and interfere with the pattern on the floor? Can the owner move a sculpture from the front lobby to another location where the work will not be seen because the owner doesn't like the finished product or because the public reacts negatively to the sculpture? If there is an obligation to keep the public art piece on site, and, if so, how long does this obligation last? One year? Five years? Until the sculpture deteriorates?

These are not easy questions to answer. The public element of the artwork implies that the owner is not free to do as he or she pleases. Moreover, the work may have been commissioned to comply with municipal development requirements and its removal or relocation may or may not have to be first approved by the municipality. Furthermore, the artist, quite apart from the municipality, may also have the contractual right to insist on continued public display of the work or sue for damages to protect his or her rights.

Well-known sculptor Robert Murray is currently involved in a dispute with the Vancouver Airport Authority that involves these issues. His sculpture, *Cumbria*, cited by the Federal Ministry of Transport in the late 1960s as part of a national program of beautification of airports, was recently dismantled and removed from the entrance to the Vancouver International Airport by the new airport operators. Murray has challenged the Airport Authority not only for moving the work without his consent, but also for the manner in which the work was dismantled, which the artist alleges has seriously damaged the integrity of the work.

Some contracts now contain specific clauses requiring the artwork to remain sited for a fixed time period after which it would appear that the owner might have the right to relocate the work.

7.   Maintenance of the artwork

To ensure the continued success of the artwork, it is critical for the owner to properly maintain it. Accordingly, it is becoming common for developers, as part of the contract, to require the artist to supply a maintenance manual giving complete instructions on proper care of the artwork. The manual should include an inventory of material used, recommendations on what products are appropriate for maintenance, any special instructions related to handling the artwork, and recommendations on the frequency of the required maintenance.

A very common maintenance problem occurs with works that incorporate running water. The Canadian climate, inadequate engineering, and the seemingly constant desire of developers to have water fountains as part of their developments, seem to have conspired to create a plague of this type of public art in Canada. Artist Susan Schelle, who created the inspired and costly salmon run water fountain at the Toronto Skydome, must wonder if water will ever fill her large fountain. Like so many other fountains, it sits waterless for the most part because of "technical difficulties."

What rights does the artist have under these circumstances to compel the owner to make the plumbing work, when plumbing is an integral part of the overall artwork?

While good maintenance is in everyone's interests, the associated costs can be substantial. Owners of public artwork should be aware of these costs and should budget for them as part of the cost of the development project.

8. If the work cannot be completed

An artwork may come to an abrupt halt in two situations: either the artist dies or becomes incapacitated, or the developer cannot complete the project. Either situation is drastic. Contracts often deal with the former, but not the latter.

If an artist dies or becomes substantially incapacitated mid-way through the creation of the work, many questions are raised: Is the developer entitled to a rebate for what has been paid to the artist to date and reject the work? Is the developer bound in the contract to complete the work? Can the work be completed as originally envisaged and with the same aesthetic result by another artist? Who owns the artwork at the stage of the artist's death?

Contracts often attempt to deal with these issues by providing that the executor of the artist's estate will work with the art consultant of the project to determine what needs to be done and whether other compatible artists can finish the work.

If a developer became insolvent, the artist is no different than any other creditor. The artist may receive no further payments and would have to decide whether to forego further work unless and until a new owner surfaces for the project.

The City of Toronto was involved in a public art project on St. Clair Avenue several years ago that raised some of these issues. The project at hand was a "peace park" supported by the local Italian community. The winning proposal was won by a team of two artists. One of the artists died midway through the proposal. The other artist did not wish to continue. The city simply hired contractors to complete a modified version of the original proposal for the park.

9. Public art contracts versus the artistic creative process

When the terms of a public art contract are drawn up, a detailed description of the artwork to be commissioned is usually included. This description establishes what the artist will produce, and what the developer will buy.

Producing the work precisely as described in the contract, however, can be an issue. Commissioned artwork can — and often does — change slightly from the time it is originally conceived to the time it reaches its final destination. The materials used might be changed to save on costs or ease future maintenance; or the developer might change the location of the work, making it necessary for the artist to adjust the dimensions. These kinds of changes are usually carefully discussed, and the consensus reached between the artist and commissioning agent must be recorded before any action is taken. If formal approval of any alterations is not obtained, the changes could be regarded as a violation of the contract by the commissioning agent who might then have grounds to refuse to pay the artist.

Toronto sculptor John McEwen created a park installation for Crown Life Assurance Company and the City of Toronto near Bloor and Church Streets. The artist's proposal called for a multi-faceted piece that included several of McEwen's trademark silhouette dogs. As the matter proceeded to installation, the artist felt the project would be aesthetically more successful if the installation had one less dog than the contract called for. The City of Toronto, however, insisted that the installation should include what was bargained for. While this case illustrates a good reason for developers to withhold full payment until the work is completed as originally agreed to, it also raises another serious issue of the degree of artistic freedom an artist should have in the continuing creation of the work as construction proceeds and whether this issue should be dealt with in the contract itself.

10. Other matters

The contractual issues discussed above are not exhaustive. Both artists and developers should seek legal input as their contracts are negotiated. As well, keep in mind that the legal costs of negotiating the contract should be budgeted as part of the cost of the creation of the work.

A final word of caution. Public artworks can be very costly and complex. Much thought should be paid to the many extraneous but important costs associated with the artwork, so the artist won't discover too late that there is so little left for profit at the end.

Remember, building an entire house may cost less than constructing a work of public art. Make a checklist of all costs associated with the project. Be realistic in budgeting and calculating how many other individuals may have to be involved. Will you need engineering help? Will you need legal help? How much will your studio space cost to rent? How much will insurance costs be? What other consultants will you need? Do you understand all the taxes you will have to pay as you construct the artwork? How much will it cost to transport the work to the installation site? What are the costs of installation?

The list can seem endless, but the more questions you think of before a contract is signed, the more likely you will realize success — both financially and artistically.

The final area that needs to be discussed within the context of the artist's contract is the provision for the conservation of the artwork. Issues such as maintenance, relocation, and de-accession need to be addressed. All too often the need to evaluate and conserve existing public art has been overshadowed by the excitement of commissioning new works of public art. The ever-present fact that change is a necessary component of the building of cities must be acknowledged and the effect of this change on individual works of art is uncertain. A recent newspaper article in the *Globe and Mail* by John Barber carries this headline: "Monument to Grandiose Intentions lies in the Mud." The reference is to Gerald Gladstone's *Universal Man,* a large bronze sculpture which was installed at the base of the CN Tower in 1975. This work had to be moved when construction on the SkyDome began in 1985. It now lies face down in the mud in the undeveloped railway lands west of the Dome. Another work by Gladstone at Pearson International Airport still stands in place, but vision of it is incomplete. The gradual extension of the buildings at the airport over the years has obliterated any possible sight lines to the work. What can be done in these circumstances? These are issues which must be addressed legally within the artist's contract.

9

ART AS PROPERTY: FAMILY LAW AND ESTATE PLANNING

by Stephen B. Smart*

Art is a unique entity made up of two facets that can — and often are — possessed separately by two people at the same time. The concept of a work of art, which includes how it looks and what ideas it expresses, is the property of the artist (see chapter 2 on copyright). The object itself, however, is something that can be sold, gifted, traded, or owned by someone else. It can appreciate and depreciate like an investment, be counted as an asset, be taxed; in short, the art object is just like any other possession you might own.

And just like any other property, arrangements regarding its ownership are affected by major events such as marriage, divorce, birth, and death.

a. FAMILY LAW AND THE ART WORLD

For the artist and art dealer whose livelihoods depend on putting so much of themselves into the public arena, it is especially important to consider how changes in marital relationships will affect their holdings. Even the collector benefits from exploring who owns what, who is responsible for what in the event of forming or dissolving a relationship, and what options an individual has for dealing with property when forming or dissolving a relationship.

In the last decade, all Canadian provinces have adopted radical changes in how property is to be dealt with when a couple separates. Provincial laws throughout Canada recognize

*With the assistance of Janet Sim, partner of Osler, Hoskin & Harcourt.

148

the validity of marriage contracts; couples can contract out of what the law would otherwise provide in such situations. Married couples have the right to design their own arrangement if they separate and are not bound by the scheme provided by law. Accordingly, anyone getting married in Canada today must consider whether they want the law to decide how their property may be affected by separation or whether they wish to design their arrangement by way of a marriage contract.

Ontario's Family Law Act, which came into force in 1986, radically altered how property is to be dealt with upon separation. Every province in Canada (except for Quebec) has similar legislation although the details vary from province to province. The discussion in this chapter is based on the Ontario legislation, which has been used as a model in some of the other provinces.

Note: While family law has evolved rapidly, the provincial laws do not yet extend fully to common law relationships nor at all to relationships between members of the same sex. This chapter discusses issues relevant to married couples. While common law partners can, in some situations, acquire certain rights, they are not addressed in this chapter.

1. General issues

The basic thrust of Ontario's Family Law Act is to recognize that marriage is a partnership. Consequently, if a married couple separates or divorces, the value of all property acquired during the period of cohabitation is shared or equalized regardless of whether or not one partner or the other put more energy into any of the traditionally recognized roles of child care, household management, or income production.

People often enter marriage with certain assets that their spouse has not helped them to acquire. To acknowledge this fact, the law recognizes that each partner should get monetary credit for the value of their net worth on entry into the marriage. However, if the value of the pre-existing assets increases during marriage, the other spouse is entitled to share the increase on separation or divorce.

The value of all assets acquired during the marriage (no matter whether it was the husband or wife who paid for them) will be shared. One important exception relates to gifts or inheritances, which are considered a windfall to an individual. They do not relate to the energy of the partnership itself. The law allows the partner of the marriage who has received a gift or inheritance to keep that asset (including any subsequent increase in value to the gift or inheritance) outside of the sharing pool.

There are two important points to keep in mind. Provincial laws (apart from any special provisions in the laws of Quebec) recognize that spouses can own property separately: what the husband owns in his name will be his and what the wife owns will be hers. What is shared is the difference in *value* of each person's net worth, not the asset itself. On separation, the person whose net worth is less can sue the other so the monetary difference in their net worth is equalized. For example, if the net worth of the wife was $200 000 and the net worth of the husband was $400 000, then the wife would be able to legally compel the husband to pay her $100 000 so that each of them would have a net worth of $300 000.

Because many couples do not have extra money available to pay the other spouse the equalization payment, other arrangements are often made. For instance, assets such as the home, business, or inventory may be sold to meet the claim put forward by the other spouse, or assets may simply be split between the husband and wife to conclude the claim.

Family law also protects the rights of the surviving spouse if, on the death of the partner, benefits are not received that match those that would have been received if the couple had separated. That is, a surviving spouse could choose to forego the benefits under the will and sue the estate of the deceased spouse for the amount he or she would have obtained on separation.

Marriage contracts dealing with any of these terms can be entered into either before or after marriage. They can be narrow documents covering a few issues, or wide documents covering a wide variety of issues. Each marriage contract is tailor-made to cover those issues relevant to the people involved.

2. Considerations for the gallery owner

A gallery business, if created and developed during the years of a marriage, is like all other assets acquired during the marriage — unless the parties had agreed otherwise in a marriage contract. That means its value will be subject to sharing.

The troublesome issue to gallery owners is that the gallery is most often regarded as a vehicle to produce a livelihood. Its object is not normally to create a business having a substantial capital value, although undoubtedly some galleries do become very valuable assets. Even in those cases, years of hard work go into building up the reputation of a gallery and it is often many years before a gallery can count on producing dependable income. When a separation occurs, the last thing a gallery owner wants is to liquidate the business in order to meet an equalization claim.

Most provincial laws give the court the discretion not to compel the sale of the gallery if it is the sole asset of the spouses and would cause severe economic hardship affecting the future economic viability of the gallery. In such cases, the court could order payments to be made from the business over time in installments, but usually no longer than a ten-year period.

Another approach to equalization is to transfer 50% of the interest in the gallery business to the other spouse. This alternative is not particularly appealing because separation implies a rift in relations and splitting the gallery could mean continuing unhappy relations.

A marriage contract that states that the value of the gallery will not be included as part of the assets to be equalized is perhaps the best preventative measure from the viewpoint of the gallery owner. Income produced from the gallery would not be affected by this kind of restriction unless further dealt with in the contract.

As a compromise, some gallery owners might consider a marriage contract that simply states that while the value of the gallery might be included for the purpose of calculating the equalization payment, under no circumstances will the claiming spouse become an owner of the business nor in any way will any settlement be able to interfere or affect the proper management or operation of the business.

If the value of a gallery does become part of the separation negotiations between husband and wife, one of the major questions will be how to value an art gallery. Will it be valued as a going concern? How much goodwill is associated in the gallery? How should the inventory be valued? To what extent is the gallery simply a vehicle to produce income having no other capital value?

These are tough questions, the answers to which may lie in the particular nature and quality of the specific gallery. Expert appraisers should be consulted to address this issue. A gallery owner may wish to have a marriage contract simply to establish the value of the gallery as of the date of marriage and to agree on how the gallery will be valued in the future so the spouses will not argue later on these important issues.

3. Considerations for the artist

An artist's inventory — the body of unsold artwork that exists on the date of separation — is an asset to be valued for the purpose of calculating equalization rights. In the eyes of the law, an artist having an inventory of artwork is no different than a manufacturer of widgets having to share the value of that product with his or her spouse on separation.

This raises practical problems for artists. Most artists do not think of inventory as capital — each work is simply viewed as a source of current or future income. Yet, on separation the artist may have to either turn over 50% of current inventory or pay 50% of its value. But how is the inventory to be valued? It is one thing to know what any individual work of art is priced at (if it sells). It is quite another proposition to say that an artist's inventory at a given moment in time is the sum of all the retail prices.

It can be argued that the inventory should be discounted substantially in value simply because there is never a market for the entire inventory at any given point in time. Furthermore the value of the inventory to the artist, if he or she is represented by a gallery, is only 50% of the retail value less any other appropriate net costs.

What does the spouse do with all this new art? Can the spouse take the treasure trove to a different gallery that is in competition with the artist's chosen gallery? If the spouse does not take the art but instead looks for a monetary adjustment, what resources does an artist have to pay his or her spouse?

An artist concerned about these issues might consider entering into a marriage contract. Here are three issues that the marriage contract should address:

(a) The spouse will have no claim to the artist's inventory (or its value) on separation

(b) If the inventory is to be valued for the purpose of equalization, the formula that will be used to calculate the valuation

(c) If the inventory is to be included in the equalization calculation, under no circumstances will the claimant spouse get ownership of a share of the inventory or immediate payment for 50% of the value of the work. Instead the parties may agree that the spouse will be entitled to 50% of the net value of the artist's interest in the work only if and when inventory from that artwork is sold.

Experience shows that many spouses of artists do not pursue their claim to include inventory in the negotiations following separation simply because of the difficulties raised above and because it is recognized that inventory is really future income, which raises the issue of support.

Many artists trade works of art with fellow artists. This habit raises the issue of the status of these works in the artist's collection on separation. If the artists traded works as gifts to each other, then the artwork is exempt from sharing with their spouses on separation. If the works were exchanged because they were of equal value rather than gifts, then it is arguable that the value of works should be included in the artist's net worth for the purpose of sharing with his or her spouse.

4. Considerations for the collector

Art collections are often the result of a joint family endeavor. In these circumstances, sharing the value of the collection on separation means a sorting out process so each spouse ends up with a fair share of work.

There are a number of common techniques to accomplish an equitable result. Once appraisals have been obtained from a qualified appraiser, the spouses may simply divide the collection in two by referring to the value of works. Alternatively, one spouse can make two lists of approximate equal value and then let the other be the first to choose one of the lists. The spouses can then barter between themselves to iron out any further adjustments in the two lists if they wish.

Even if the collection has been put together by only one spouse, or if there is a desire for the collection to be kept intact, without a marriage contract exempting the artwork from sharing, the value of the collection will be included in the calculation of any equalization claim. This occurs regardless of who paid for the works, but ownership of the collection will remain with the person who paid.

A marriage contract can prevent unwanted division of an art collection. The contract should state that the spouses agree that the value of the collection can be included for the purpose of equalization, but under no circumstances will it be broken up or divided, and that it will remain in the possession of the collector. It may save later acrimony to establish in a contract the value of the collection as of the date of marriage and a formula for the future valuation of the collection.

Art collections are often inherited. If a collection is inherited *before* marriage, its value at the time of marriage will be exempted from an equalization claim. Any increase in the value of the collection from the date of marriage to the date of separation, however, will be shared. The value of an art collection inherited *after* the marriage is also exempt from sharing, and any increase in value of the work from the date of its receipt until the date of separation is also exempt.

For persons who may be thinking of gifting a collection or a portion of a collection to a son or daughter, the timing of the gift is significant for the very same reason. If the gift is made after the collector's child has married, then the whole value of the work will be exempt. Gifts made before the marriage entitles the child to an exemption for the value of the work as of the date of marriage, but an increase in value after marriage must be shared with his or her spouse.

b. ESTATE PLANNING AND THE ART WORLD

For the artist and collector, the object of estate planning is to appropriately provide for works of art or a collection according to personal wishes and in such a way that taxes are minimized. Appropriate planning involves many considerations, including the following:

(a) Passing artwork on to the next generation

(b) Deciding whether a collection should be split up or allowed to remain intact

(c) Deciding the eventual destination and ownership of the collection or art inventory

(d) Determining whether there is any interest in using the collection as an educational tool

(e) Exploring how taxes can be minimized on assets both while living and after death

(f) Establishing whether artwork should be gifted or sold to reduce outstanding debts or other estate liabilities

(g) Managing inventory to maintain appropriate price levels and to increase the reputation of the work and its importance to the cultural life of the community

Four of the more common techniques for dealing with these issues are —

(a) establishing gifts,

(b) setting up trusts ("inter vivos trusts"),

(c) planning the estate through the last will and testament, and

(d) naming an art executor.

1. Gifts

An artist or collector might want to plan to give some or all of a collection as part of an estate plan. To "qualify" as a gift for the purposes of tax and legal considerations, the work must —

(a) be given freely and without payment,

(b) be physically transferred to the recipient, who becomes the new owner (although there may be cases where the work is not transferred for practical reasons, but the gift is still deemed complete), and

(c) be accepted by the recipient. In other words, you cannot make a gift to another without the recipient being aware of the transfer and indicating his or her agreement to accept the gift.

The giver must also be of sound mind at the time when he or she gives the work.

It is possible to give a work to another person or art institution but retain possession of the work for either a fixed number of years or the balance of one's lifetime. This permits the donor the continued use and enjoyment of the work and, at the same time, makes the gift (and its tax benefits) effective immediately. Many museums and galleries are reluctant to accept gifts subject to such a condition, but a number of other galleries have active "promised gift programs" as part of their activities to attract new donations.

You can also give someone the right to possess, use, and enjoy a work of art for a specified time period. In this case, it is not the work itself that is being gifted. When the time period expires, the work must be returned to the original owner.

In both the situations described above, the transaction should be documented to avoid disputes regarding possession or ownership. A simple letter of agreement that describes the details of the arrangement is sufficient.

To avoid or minimize the tax consequences of gifting, a person may choose to gift artwork to either a registered charitable institution or to a qualified institution authorized to receive gifts of artworks under the Cultural Property Export and Import Act. Canadian tax laws encourage gifts being made to cultural or charitable institutions by reducing the taxes otherwise payable by the person making the gift. (See chapter 10 for more on cultural property donations and chapter 11 for more on the tax implications of gifts.)

2. Trusts

A trust is created when property is transferred by one person to another (the trustee) who holds the property for the benefit of a third person (the beneficiary). Trusts differ from gifts in that the absolute ownership of the property, and sometimes its use and enjoyment, is postponed for a certain period of time from the ultimate beneficiaries. The terms of a trust are generally documented in a trust deed or an indenture.

An artist or collector might consider using a trust in three situations. First, an artist or collector might establish a trust to dispose of artwork so that it does not constitute part of his or her estate on death (thereby avoiding probate fees). Subject to considering the tax consequences of doing so, the artist or collector could still retain some control over the trust by acting as a trustee.

Second, a trust is useful when an artist or collector wants to provide a beneficiary with the use and enjoyment of artwork during the beneficiary's lifetime but also wants to pass absolute ownership of the work to other beneficiaries on the death of the first beneficiary. For example, a collector might allow a child the use of an artwork during the child's lifetime, but when the child dies, ownership of the work would pass to a public gallery.

Finally, trusts are useful when an artist or collector wants to provide someone with the use and enjoyment of artwork, but is concerned that that person is not capable of managing, maintaining, and preserving the artwork. In this situation, the trustees could ensure the welfare of the artwork.

Trustees are obliged to file annual income tax returns to report the income in the trust (if any) and to maintain accounts for the management of the trust property.

158

3. Last will and testament

The cornerstone of estate planning is the last will and testament. The most obvious reason to have a will is to ensure that your estate is distributed as you wish and not according to a legislated scheme. Dying without a will is known as dying intestate.

In a will, a person can include specific bequests or legacies as well as provide for the general bulk or residue of the estate. These bequests or legacies are comparable to making gifts while alive — the significant difference being that they take effect only on death. Bequests or legacies can be made to relatives or friends. They can also be made to charitable institutions or institutions qualifying under the Cultural Property Export and Import Act. These latter forms of bequests generally provide the estate with the same tax relief as would be provided to an individual had the gift been made while the person was still alive. An important restriction, however, is that it is not always possible to fully utilize the resulting tax credit (see chapter 11).

The Income Tax Act restricts the use of donation receipts to 20% of a person's income in the year. Donations that exceed this restriction, however, can be carried forward and claimed on future tax returns for up to five years. On death, the excess donation may only be carried back one year.

While gifts to charitable institutions are less complicated, an artist or collector may wish to make any gifts to cultural institutions conditional on the estate obtaining the full tax credits available under the Cultural Property Export and Import Act. In this case, it is wise to provide for an alternative beneficiary because the gift may not qualify under the act. If an alternate beneficiary is not established, a rejected gift will fall into the residue of the estate and be distributed to the persons entitled under the will to the residue.

A second reason for having a will is to minimize taxes payable on death. The tax treatment for an artist's inventory

159

will be different from the treatment for an art collector, who was not in the business of selling art. (This important distinction is discussed in chapter 11.) It may be possible to reduce taxes by considering and implementing a gifting program and a trust arrangement either before death or within the terms of a will, and by deciding which beneficiaries get what property.

4. Naming an art executor

The main concern in estate planning for an artist or collector is determining what exactly he or she wants done with the art inventory or collection upon death. Because of the special nature of these assets and because art is a part of the cultural life of the community, special issues and concerns arise. Chapter 2 of this book describes the very special rights of copyright, moral rights, and exhibition rights artists have. Many of these rights continue for a number of years following death. Estate executors must be aware of these special rights which accompany the works of art they are responsible for managing.

When preparing a will, the naming of an executor (the person who will administer and manage the deceased's estate), is critically important. After the initial administration is complete, if there are ongoing responsibilities imposed by the will, the executor becomes known as the trustee, and not everyone has the special knowledge or sensitivity required to deal with the issues of art management. Very often those closest to the artist and collector know little or nothing about the intricacies of either the artwork or the art world, and therefore are inappropriate choices for the role of executor. The dealer representing an artist may not be a good choice because there may be a conflict of interest between the gallery owner and the beneficiaries of the estate.

For this reason, artists and collectors often appoint an "art executor" — someone who has special expertise in the art area and who is independent of any possible conflict of interest. This individual has responsibility for the administration of the artwork only. The artist or collector can then appoint someone else to act as executor of the balance of the estate.

When arranging for an executor, it is important to keep in mind how his or her services will be compensated. Most provinces provide for a small percentage of the value of the estate (usually around 5%) at death plus a care and management fee based on a percentage of the average annual market value of the assets under administration.

If these costs sound steep, just remember that Pablo Picasso, one of the greatest artists (and collectors) of this century, died without a will. Poor Pablo would probably turn in his grave to realize what a savings it would have been to pay executors their fee rather than see the millions spent in legal wrangling following his death.

An art executor should be someone who knows and understands the importance of the collection or the significance of the artist's work. The executor should be someone who understands issues relating to appropriate pricing of works of art and the market for the particular artwork or collection, the tax implications involved in the disposition of artwork, and the possible need for appropriate publication of catalogues and educational material related to the artwork or collection. The executor should not be someone who has a conflict of interest with the beneficiaries of the estate or be in a position to personally gain in any way to the detriment of the beneficiaries. He or she should also be someone who knows, subject to the terms of the will, when it is appropriate to wind up this part of the deceased's estate.

One of the most fascinating stories from the art world in the seventies involved the estate of the famous American artist, Mark Rothko. Following his death in 1970, Rothko's will was probated appointing three executors to manage this very valuable and important estate: his dealer, an artist friend, and a professor. In very short order, two of the executors, Rothko's dealer and artist friend, had sold a large part of the estate inventory to a corporation controlled by one of the executors. The executors' actions, clearly motivated by the desire to make a personal profit, were in direct conflict with their duty to act fairly to the beneficiaries of the estate. When the case found its way to court, the individuals were relieved of their responsibilities regarding the estate and fined substantial amounts for their flagrant failure to act in good faith.

The third executor was in a different position. The professor had not participated in selling the works to the corporation. He had also voiced some concern about the sale.

For the court these measures were not enough. The third executor had become aware of the sale but had not taken active steps to oppose it or prevent it from happening. The court, therefore, placed a substantial fine on this "passive executor" and also removed him from continuing to act in the estate. The court stated, as a warning to future executors who become aware of wrongdoing, "He could not close his eyes, remain passive, or move with unconcern in the face of the obvious loss to be visited upon the estate by participation in those business arrangements and then shelter himself behind the claimed counsel of an attorney."

Artists and collectors must recognize that the art executor will be much better equipped to deal with the artwork comprising the estate if they keep the following documents or information readily available:

(a) A complete record of the inventory of the artwork, including titles of work, year of execution, and the medium and size of the work

(b) A description of where the work is located

(c) As much documentary material as is available relating to the acquisition of the work in the case of collected work

(d) Copies of any appraisals that may exist or other documents relating to a description of the value of the work

(e) Information about any tax treatment that may relate to any particular work

An artist's legal relationship with his or her art dealer normally expires on the death of the artist. The artist may, therefore, wish to communicate by way of a letter to the executor accompanying the will, his or her preferences regarding which gallery should be engaged by the art executor following death. While the executor is not legally bound to such an expression of wishes, it does give important direction and advice to the art executor.

5. Duties of the executor

Following the death of the artist or collector, the art executor will have many responsibilities. In the case of an artist's estate, he or she must differentiate between the inventory of artwork available and that which is part of the artist's private collection, as the two will be handled differently. The executor must also ensure that all financial documents relating to the artwork are in place, including updated appraisals. The administration of copyright is another ongoing duty.

Most important, the executor must determine how to continue to market the artist's work. For example, he or she must decide what pricing adjustments should be made and whether to place the work with the gallery that represented the artist during his or her life. Very often, of course, the executor's decision will be to continue to work with the established dealer who is familiar with the artist's work and who understands the market opportunities for that work.

Handling a collector's estate is similar. The executor must make sure that up-to-date inventory and financial records are available and, if the collection is to be donated or sold, must determine the value of the collection.

In both cases, it is important for the executor to ensure that the artwork is adequately insured during the period of art management or risk being found negligent in the duty of providing adequate security and safety for the works. Obtaining appraisals of the collection is important because probate fees related to the estate are based on the fair market value of the collection.

Finally, the executor should keep an eye on archival bibliographical material, which might include notes, records, letters, articles, studio material, etc. This type of material can be donated to a museum or archival resource for future study. Many institutions may welcome archival material, and such a gift may produce tax benefits for the estate.

10

GIFTING CULTURAL PROPERTY

A conversation with Jeffrey Spalding
and Stephen B. Smart

In Canada, laws are in place to encourage and foster the growth of public collections by providing tax incentives for donations of art. There are two streams for gifting works. One is the regular straight gift to charitable institutions, which are governed solely by the provisions of the Income Tax Act (ITA). The second stream concerns gifts to designated institutions (a narrower group than the charitable institutions), which are governed by both the ITA and the Cultural Property Export and Import Act (CPE & IA).

The laws are not intended to be a vehicle by which people can create wealth. But they do recognize that the value of cultural property escalates over time and that, therefore, there is opportunity for people to do well financially through the process of donation.

The following conversation with Jeffrey Spalding, Director of the University of Lethbridge Art Gallery, reviews the issues important to donors, institutions, and artists when considering cultural property.

a. UNDERSTANDING THE RULES AND PROCEDURE

SS: What is cultural property?

JS: In fine arts, cultural property is obvious. But cultural property is also museum-style objects, artifacts, books, furnishings, antiques, etc. Cultural property is the term the federal government uses when designating objects of this type to be of national significance and importance.

SS: What kind of benefits does the Income Tax Act offer someone who is wanting to gift work?

JS: Under the Income Tax Act, you may make charitable gifts (money or artwork) of up to 20% of your taxable income in any year and receive a tax deduction for that donation. However, these gifts are subject to capital gains.

SS: How is a gift that is considered cultural property under the CPE & IA different from a straight gift?

JS: If a work of art is certified by the Cultural Property Review Board, then the donor is offered a tax certificate that allows the entire appraised value of the work to be deducted. So, if work is appraised at $10 000, then you may use that $10 000 as a tax credit to diminish the ultimate amount of tax that you otherwise would have to pay in the year of the donation. The second advantage is that once it is certified, any capital gains otherwise payable is waived.

SS: I know that being certified means that the Cultural Property Review Board, which is coordinated by the federal Ministry of Communications, issues a certificate to declare the gift as cultural property. But what exactly is the Board? What is its role?

JS: The Board's responsibility is to decide on behalf of the government when it is appropriate to offer enhanced tax advantages to taxpayers as they may apply to various artworks and artifacts.

SS: What are the Board's requirements for certification?

JS: To start with, the recipient institution must be a designated institution. So it limits who is eligible to receive gifts under this act. Designated institutions are cultural institutions, and they have certain expectations of them. In order to qualify for this donation the institutions have to file an application for certification on behalf of the donor and demonstrate why this particular work should be designated.

SS: How does a collector or artist know which is and which is not a designated institution?

JS: Well, you are simply going to ask. There isn't a big plaque on their door. But most of the larger public institutions in the country that have a collection are designated.

SS: Who prepares the application for certification of a donation?

JS: At the University of Lethbridge Art Gallery, we always do. However, the donor or vendor can do it. In order for a work to be certified as cultural property for income tax purposes, the application has to include a description of the work: its history, condition, provenance, and exhibition record.

Another requirement is that the recipient institution must provide a declaration of authenticity to the Board. The institution must either have someone authenticate the object or have someone in their institution who is qualified and able to declare the object to be authentic. With contemporary material this is usually relatively simple because the work is often known to have come directly from the artist or the authorized dealers. In this case the resident opinion within the institution can simply be used to declare its authenticity.

In the case of School of Paris material, 1920s Degas and Picassos, that kind of thing, the potential for forgeries or fakes is very real. Real expertise must be sought and the authority on those matters must be cited.

The application must also demonstrate the work's outstanding significance and national importance. It must say, "this particular work is by an artist of note and record," and describe in what way this particular thing has some close association with Canadian history or culture or pertinence to the cultural purposes of the nation.

Some of the smaller institutions and the smaller communities mistake the notion of national importance. It would be clear what the national importance would be of a member of the Group of Seven. We know what it means in terms of the nation's history. But in every smaller region of the country there are individuals whose contributions to cultural life and benefits are extraordinary within that area.

It is possible and appropriate for arguments to be made that artwork and objects of importance to a local region contribute significantly to our collective national heritage. Canada is, after all, a collection of regional areas. So if something is of great importance to the history of the cultural development in southern Alberta, I have every right to argue that it is important to our nation. Time and time again, the Cultural Property Board has upheld that observation as correct. A small institution therefore shouldn't shy away from considering a gift of work which on its face has regional history or influence.

SS: Can an artwork from outside the country be important to Canada's national culture?

JS: Art is an international language. Canada considers itself to be a multicultural society. Therefore art objects that pertain to the history of civilization are of value and importance for Canadians to be aware of and come in contact with. So you know, whether it be Chinese artifacts, Persian miniatures, African art, or international British contemporary art, you can say that it is important to this nation.

Another angle for international artists is to establish their possible relationship with Canada in their application for cultural certification. For instance, if you were to offer a work of art by Milton Avery, you would point out that this important American artist spent time and worked in Canada, and the particular work was not only known to Canadian artists but exhibited in Canada. Avery's work was acknowledged and admired and used as a point of reference for many significant artists of note in our own country. You might also give examples of which Canadian artists those might be. This gives some context to the artist and the work.

SS: If a work is of national significance to one institution, is it necessarily of national importance to another institution?

JS: The words "national importance" are to be broadly interpreted. For example, if the National Gallery of Canada wants to apply for certification for a high edition Victor Vasarely print, the Board may ask: "Victor Vasarely is an acknowledged artist but does the National Gallery really need to offer a certification certificate for this rather less than wonderful object?"

However, if you are in a small museum that has a very modest collection, you might be able to reasonably argue that this object gives your audience some access to a type of art that they otherwise do not have access to and, therefore, the Board would find it acceptable to approve this gift.

There is another criterion. The recipient institution also must demonstrate how the object is of value to its mandate. This is an important thing to do. If we were to walk through the case of Milton Avery as an offer to the University of Lethbridge, someone might well wonder of what possible value is a work by Milton Avery, an East Coast American artist, to a small town university collection in the prairies of western Canada? Why is that the right institution to receive that object?

We must demonstrate a number of things: one, that we are collecting American art of that time period; two, that in western Canada, artists have spent an enormous amount of time reflecting upon the career of Milton Avery and, therefore, their own work has a very special relationship with that work; and, three, we have either relatable works by the same artist, or relatable artists to Avery in our collection of the same time period, or works that emanate from that time period.

SS: A fair amount of work falls to the institutions.

JS: I think that it usually staggers small institutions as they start things out — or institutions that haven't done a lot of it. They just say, "How are we ever going to be able to provide all of these things?" However, if you keep in mind that the majority of institutions in the country, even the larger ones, don't have any acquisition money to purchase works, donations are the most important acquisition method of today and of the future, I am sure. They are, to put it simply, the only game in town.

SS: Staff have to recognize that coordinating these applications is a significant part of their jobs.

JS: True, and they simply can't think of it as something that deflects them from their work. It is their work. The successful institutions are those that have been able to

170

recognize that coordinating applications for certification of cultural property is their job. It is a service that they provide on behalf of those making these items available to Canadian taxpayers, and they must make the process as easy and as professional as possible.

b. FROM THE DONOR'S POINT OF VIEW

SS: How does the gifting process commence?

JS: The donor writes to an institution to determine whether that institution is interested in receiving a proposed donation. Usually, that letter sets out any conditions to be attached to the proposed donations. Common conditions include that the gift receive certification status under the CPE & IA and that the appraisal comes in at a figure within a range that the donor feels the work is worth. If the conditions can be met, the gift stands.

However, if you place conditions on your offer of gift, then legally, the work is not gifted until all the conditions are lifted. Let me walk you through this for a second. When you offer an unconditional gift, you are entitled to apply whatever tax benefits ultimately occur to your return in the year in which the offer was made. So if you make the unconditional offer of gift by midnight December 31 of a given year, then even though it may take many months to process, you are eligible to file a supplementary tax return and apply it back to the year in which you made the actual unconditional offer of gift.

If, however, you write to me before midnight on December 31 of this year to offer work as a potential gift subject to conditions, and if I cannot remove those conditions before December 31 of that year, the work is not legally gifted or transacted in that year. It can only be transacted when the conditions are lifted.

SS: The year for which you receive a tax receipt is the year you make an unconditional gift or, if you have placed conditions on your gift, the year in which these conditions are lifted. But the process of accepting the gift, of putting it before the Cultural Property Review Board for certification must take a long time. There must be many occasions when matters come before the Board before the end of December but do not get resolved until the new year.

JS: People who are considering making offers of gift through the certification process must realize that it takes a long time to do it. After you write your letter of offer, it takes some time to get a reply from the institution. Usually the offer has to be approved by either the institution's acquisition committee or Board.

Next, the institution either has to receive the object or a photo of the object, which again takes more time. After they receive the object they inspect it, determine its provenance, and check its condition to confirm whether or not they want to proceed with the gift. Then they photograph the object and apply for appraisal.

An appraisal can often take eight weeks. By then four to six months may have passed. Only when appraisals are in hand together with all those other bits and pieces of the application for certification, can it all go to the Board for certification. You cannot send in an incomplete application with support material to follow. It must be sent complete.

The Board meets approximately four times a year and considers all requests for receipts. It is not unusual for the process to take eight or nine months from the time that you actually make an offer to an institution to the time they actually provide you with a certificate. So the donor should keep in mind that if it is important to receive a tax certificate well in advance of an April filing date, he or she should make the offer early in the year.

SS: Is it possible for an individual to make a gift of artwork to your institution but still keep possession of the artwork for the balance of his or her lifetime?

JS: Yes, that's a gift with lifetime interest. It is for objects of incredible cultural as well as monetary value. Most institutions do not like to receive objects with encumbrances on them. However, some institutions are willing to go through the process just to secure an object that they wish to acquire in the future. You, as a collector, may have a fabulous work that is in your collection that you want to place now. You know that you have got the institution in mind where it should go and you also have the opportunity.

Another aspect of gifting is that there is always an element of risk or window or opportunity because institutions change leadership and direction; all sorts of things can change. It may be that once the perfect place for certain work would have been an institution that had always collected that kind of work. But recently they may have changed direction, and the new group may decide they don't want to take that kind of work anymore. Sometimes a work may be worth a lot of money at one time but not at another. The value could plummet.

This presents an opportunity to place the work. It's economically advantageous to place it at this time, but the donor may be so enamored with it he or she doesn't want to give up physical possession. That is where the idea of gifting with lifetime interest comes in. You an make an offer to gift something at the time subject to an agreement that the work stays with you for your lifetime. It is deeded; it is given to the institution, its title is turned over, it now belongs to the institution.

SS: But physical possession remains with the donor?

JS: Yes. Gifting with a lifetime interest allows you to keep the object in your home or in your possession subject to a reasonable call for legitimate museum-style exhibitions from time to time. A prior arrangement has been made between the institution and the donor to loan the work back to the donor once the gift is made.

SS: What if an artist or collector has something of substantial value and wants to gift it, but also wants to sell part of it? He or she wants a transaction that provides part tax receipt and part cash. Can you do that?

JS: No. You can only do one thing or the other, but not a combination. You can't take an object that has a genuine value of $100 000 and sell half to me for $50 000 and ask me for a tax receipt for the other $50 000. But you could do a gift/sale business of two objects, one of which is gifted and one of which is sold.

SS: Are tax benefits available to a taxpayer who sells work to a designated cultural institution?

JS: Yes, if it is a work of national significance and the recipient institution is willing to file its report for you, then even if you are selling it, you can receive the benefits of certification. So if you sell a Group of Seven painting to a designated institution, you can still have the Board rule on whether or not it qualifies as an object of national significance and importance. If approved, this would waive your capital gains tax otherwise payable on the artwork.

174

c. APPRAISING THE ARTWORK

SS: One of the fundamental issues in cultural property relates to appraisals of the artwork. How does the process of obtaining appraisals work?

JS: To receive tax benefit, the object must be accompanied by an appraisal, and the appraisal must be acceptable to the Cultural Property Review Board in determining the fair market value of the work. Any single donation, whether it be one object or a combination of objects, whose total appraised value is less than $10 000, may only require one appraisal under the current guidelines. These guidelines change from time to time.

The appraisal must be done by someone who is qualified to give opinion on the work in question. Previously, it was only members of the Professional Art Dealers Association of Canada (PADAC) or its like association, internationally, who were qualified to give values. Now it is extended to other forms of scholars or people knowledgeable in the market.

SS: Who has the ultimate responsibility for deciding the fair market value of the work?

JS: Determining fair market value is a matter between the donor and the Cultural Review Board, with institutions sometimes being caught in the middle. In law, and this is fairly recent, the Board has been given the legal authority to settle this issue.

SS: As an institution, what are the procedures you would normally follow in obtaining appraisals?

JS: For pragmatic purposes, the University of Lethbridge has adopted a policy which I think is becoming standard across the country. We undertake to seek the appraisals on behalf of the donor, although it is legally the donor's responsibility not only to obtain the appraisal, but to pay for it. We have found that occasional or first-time donors do not want to learn how to do all this for one occasion. They do not need the bother and stress. So most of the recipient institutions take on the business and the responsibility of seeking the evaluation and appraisal on behalf of the donor.

SS: How do institutions handle the sensitive issue of asking a donor to pay for the cost of the appraisal?

JS: Appraisals and the cost of shipping works can cost a lot a money. If an institution wants to be in the business of building up its collections, they have to be prepared to set aside resources to cover those costs. It may, however, not have enough resources to set aside. So institutions may have no choice but to be straightforward with a potential donor and say, "We would love to have it. However, we do not have money to do this so if you are able to pay for its appraisal and/or its shipping or its other covering costs then we would be delighted to have the object and make the application. By the way, those costs are also tax deductible to you."

SS: If they are paid to your institution.

JS: That is right. If the estimate is that the appraisal for an object and its shipping costs will amount to $1 200, the donor might decide to make a money donation of that amount to the institution and receive a tax receipt for it in return.

SS: It wouldn't be uncommon for a donor to have a strong view regarding the value of the potential donation.

JS: That is true. If the work isn't at least appraised at this level, the donor sometimes feels that it is not of any value to consider proceeding with the donation. In this case, the person may rather just hold onto the work for the time being.

SS: Will only one appraisal suffice in all cases?

JS: For gifts in excess of $10 000, whether it be an individual object or groups of objects, you must provide either one PADAC appraisal, which is accepted as a group appraisal, or alternatively at least two appraisals. In the latter situation, the Cultural Property Review Board usually takes the two appraisals and averages them. It also can take the lower value, rather than the higher value. There is no particular expectation or standard.

SS: Which is the most accepted choice for appraisals — PADAC, or two separate appraisals?

JS: The most obvious and preferred route is to provide a PADAC appraisal. It is the one which, in my experience, has caused the least number of questions to have to be reanswered by reappraisals or further substantiations.

SS: What does the Board do with the submitted appraisals?

JS: The Cultural Review Board has the right and the responsibility to adjudicate appraisals to determine whether in their opinion they are fair and reasonable. If the Board feels uncomfortable with them, they may ask for further substantiation of the appraisals, additional appraisals, or they may instead offer you their own view of the value of the work under condition. For example, you have an appraisal of this object at $15 000. The Board may simply reply that this appears high and their experts have suggested an alternate value of $10 000. In this case, your donor might decide to accept the value, instruct you to enter into negotiations, or reject and withdraw his or her gift.

SS: What remedies does the donor have if he or she is unsatisfied with the final position taken by the Board?

JS: Steps are being taken to provide an appeal process to the Federal Court of Canada if a donor cannot accept the position the Board has taken. I don't know if it has actually been constituted yet. The appeal process has just been announced.

d. THE CULTURAL PROPERTY REPATRIATION PROGRAM

SS: How does a public gallery get involved in the repatriation program under the CPE & IA?

JS: Let's look at the situation where either the institution becomes aware, or someone makes the institution aware, that there is an outstanding object of national significance currently owned outside of the country and for sale.

The institution makes an application for repatriation. Basically it is the same sort of process as applying for certification. You have to demonstrate in what way the object is of national significance and importance. You should also be certain to demonstrate the uniqueness of the object that is being repatriated.

An example of this process might be the University of Lethbridge's application to acquire a fabulous Jack Bush painting that was in a private collection in the United States. Because there are a lot of Jack Bush paintings in Canada, how could we argue that public money should be spent on repatriating another one? So it had to be a matter of demonstrating in what way this work was of special significance and worthy of being repatriated.

In this particular case, we repatriated a painting called *Indian Red Low,* a painting from 1965 which is a companion work to Dazzle Red currently located at the Art Gallery of Ontario. It had been sent off to the Sao Paulo Bienale in 1967 or 1968. It went directly from the artist's studio without ever having been exhibited in Canada and was bought directly out of the Sao Paulo exhibition by an American collector. It never came back to Canada. *Indian Red Low* was always thought of as one of Bush's finest paintings.

The case that we made was that it was a work of outstanding quality, related to the most admired period of the artist's work, was a companion piece to the other truly remarkable painting of Bush's career, was chosen by Bush to represent himself at the same time as he had *Dazzle Red* in his studio, which indicates his own admiration for the painting, and was one of those works that has gone on to be of such repute and importance in the discussion about the evolution of Canada's history.

SS: The other aspect of cultural property control relates to artworks leaving Canada to be sold internationally. What controls exist to prevent works of national importance from leaving Canada?

JS: By law, persons owning works of national importance are not entitled to take them outside Canada for the purpose of sale without an export permit. If a work is of national importance, the Cultural Property Review Board will not authorize the issuance of a permit unless it is clear there are no buyers within Canada to purchase the work at its fair market price.

While the act puts very real restrictions on the mobility of cultural objects, the owner can hardly complain if a buyer is found for the work at a satisfactory price within Canada. Apart from all the bureaucratic red tape and the possible lost time to the owner, everyone seems to win in this scenario. If no purchaser is found, the owner will of course feel completely abused — the work of art will have been tied up for a year or two with bureaucratic wrangling and he or she may have lost other opportunities for the work apart from feeling that his or her freedoms have been interfered with. But if no buyer is found, the Cultural Property Review Board will have to permit the work to leave the country.

SS: How does the process work if an owner of a work that may be of national importance packs the work in the car and heads south across the border?

JS: Very often what happens is that an owner is stopped at the border and the customs official notes that it is a work of art. The customs officer may decide that he or she needs a ruling on whether the work is of national importance. The Cultural Review Board can issue a temporary order requiring the work be held for a hearing while they investigate further into whether the work is of national importance or not. If there is a preliminary view that the work is of national importance, then the process begins to attempt to find a Canadian buyer.

SS: I take it the process only relates to work that an owner intends to sell outside the country.

JS: It is only for that purpose. It has nothing to do with exhibitions or whatever. It just has to do with things that are being sold outside Canada.

11

TAXES, TAXES, AND MORE TAXES

by Malcolm Welch
with Michael Burch and Garth Steele

Unfortunately, no book dealing with art and the law can avoid the unpopular topic of taxes. In Canada, the most pervasive laws are contained in the Income Tax Act and the act levying the GST.

Both of these taxes apply to the transfer of ownership of a work of art. While that in itself is a simple concept, the actual application varies depending on the transferor (artist, dealer, or collector), method of transfer (sale, barter, or gift), and the status of the transferor at the time of transfer (individual, dead or alive, or a corporation). However, in nearly all cases, for tax purposes a work of art is a commodity and is, therefore, treated like all other commodities traded commercially.

This chapter does not provide a how-to guide for tax return preparation, or even a comprehensive review of all the applicable rules and regulations. It is intended to highlight provisions of the laws that directly affect anyone concerned with the creation and/or sale or donation of works of art.

In the following sections, two chartered accountants with Welch & Co., an accountancy firm in Ottawa, answer many of the questions anyone involved in the art world may have about taxes. Michael Burch tackles the subject of income taxes (sections **a.** to **e.** below), and Garth Steele deals with the GST (section **f.**).

a. INCOME TAX AND THE ARTIST

MW: When considering income tax, is the artist the same as an independent business person manufacturing goods for re-sale?

MB: Yes. As a result, the artist is subject to the same restrictions under the federal Income Tax Act as all independent businesses in Canada. Included in these restrictions is the concept of a "reasonable expectation of profit." That is, to be considered a business, there must be a reasonable expectation of profit. This does not mean that a profit must be generated in year one and every year thereafter, but that at some stage in the future, the activities of the artist will produce revenues in excess of costs.

Revenue Canada publishes an Information Bulletin (IT504R) which provides a detailed listing of the factors it considers in determining if a reasonable expectation of profit exists. This bulletin acknowledges that an artist may not realize a profit during his or her lifetime but may still have a reasonable expectation of profit. Being considered as a business person for income tax purposes enables the artist to charge all those costs incurred in creating the art as a deduction from income before calculating taxable income.

MW: Then, starting with the artist, a sale generates revenue. What costs and expenses can be deducted to arrive at the artist's net taxable income?

MB: Essentially, all material costs associated with producing the artwork are deductible: canvas, wood, props, film, chemicals, tools used in working the raw materials, and so on. An artist should, therefore, keep a complete record of all out-of-pocket costs paid by him or her for materials.

MW: Perhaps this is a logical place to talk about inventories. The manufacturer is required to value inventory at year-end. Is it the same for the artist?

MB: Inventory includes unsold finished goods, goods in process, and materials and supplies on hand for future production. Revenue Canada allows artists to deduct the costs associated with their inventory in the fiscal period in which such costs are incurred whether or not those costs have been used on current work. What this means is that the inventory will be carried for tax purposes at no value. This is an elective position available to the artist at his or her discretion.

By selecting this option, the artist increases the deductible expenses incurred in a fiscal period. This may result in a reduction of the artist's reportable earnings or an increase in the reportable loss. Either case results in lower taxes payable. There is no prescribed "election" form to file. To benefit from this provision, the artist files the income tax return indicating that the closing inventory value is nil.

MW: What else can be deducted?

MB: An artist can deduct all indirect expenses involved: studio rent, telephone, and other utilities, and all other expenses incurred that can reasonably be attributed to earning income by creating and selling art. The expenses must be claimed in the year in which they are incurred.

Furthermore, artists are eligible to claim capital cost allowance (depreciation) on fixed assets used to create art — like photographic and darkroom equipment or computer equipment. The amount of capital cost allowance varies. Generally, tools (costing in excess of $200) and equipment can be written off at 20% per year on the declining balance basis (but only 50% of that amount may be claimed in the year in which the asset is acquired). Small tools costing less than $200 each should not be capitalized but written off as an expense in the year of acquisition. It should be noted that computer software is in a class entitled to a 100% depreciation rate. Fifty percent can be claimed in the year of acquisition and the balance in the next taxation year.

MW: You mention studio rent. What about the artist who maintains a studio at home?

MB: The artist who maintains a studio in the home can deduct all the direct costs related to that studio (e.g., a separate studio phone line), as well as a portion of some of the other household expenses incurred. However, to qualify, the home studio must represent the artist's principal place of business. Proportionate shares of the following household expenses can be deducted: rent, heat, hydro, repairs and maintenance, mortgage interest, property taxes, and insurance.

These "household" expenses are only deductible against revenue generated from the artist's business. Unlike the other direct and indirect deductible expenses, "household" expenses cannot be used to create a loss from the artist's business which could be used to offset other income.

If the home is owned by the artist, I do not generally advise that it be depreciated like other fixed assets because under the current provisions of the act, an individual can realize a capital gain on the disposition of his or her principal residence without incurring personal tax.

If significant structural changes are undertaken to create a "business use" space, the residence no longer qualifies 100% as a principal residence. Under these circumstances a change of use occurs, and the taxpayer is deemed to have disposed of a portion of the property for the proportional share of the fair market value at the date of conversion. This may result in a capital gain which would qualify for the principal residence exemption. Any subsequent gain realized on a disposal of the property would be proportionately subject to tax.

The artist can claim capital cost allowance on the capital costs of the converted portion of the property. These costs would include the proportionate cost of the original house along with the capital costs of conversion.

If the artist makes structural changes to a rented property, the costs would be considered leasehold improvements, which are available for write-off on a straight line basis over the term of the lease plus one renewal term. In any event, this term cannot be less than five years.

MW: How about other costs? Are costs of travel deductible to the artist?

MB: Travel should be claimed if the artist can reasonably argue that the travel was necessary for the creation of his or her art — painting trips, for example — or if the purpose was to create sales. Examples might be travel costs incurred to develop a sales outlet for work, to attend an out-of-town opening of the artist's work, or to submit a proposal for a possible commissioned work. In that last case the costs should be allowable whether or not the proposal was ultimately accepted.

MW: What about travel, say to New York, to see either a specific art exposition that could be directly beneficial to the artist's development or to see what developments are taking place there in his or her chosen field?

MB: Unfortunately, Canadian tax law is not black and white. In the example you have presented you could certainly argue in favor of this deduction. But almost certainly, it would be questioned by the tax department. As long as the artist is prepared to put up supporting documents and reasons, if questioned, it should be claimed and left to the department to consider its deductibility. One sure thing is that if an expense is not claimed, there's no chance of getting a tax benefit from it. Many taxpayers are afraid of the tax assessor, but this is unwarranted as long as the taxpayer has reasonable arguments to support his or her claim.

MW: If an artist is lucky enough to be included in an out-of-country show, from which no sales are anticipated, but which produces career benefits such as prestige or publicity, would travel costs be deductible?

MB: For an expense to be deductible, it must be incurred to earn income. If the artist's income earning capacity is enhanced by such a trip the amount should be deductible.

MW: Can an artist claim a net loss from his or her art against other income, such as grants, fees from teaching, or pay for any kind of work taken to supplement income?

MB: Losses incurred in the artist's business can be used to offset other income earned in the year from all sources. If a non-capital loss, which is what an operating business loss is, cannot be fully utilized in the year incurred, it can be carried back up to three years to offset income of those years. Or, if it's more advantageous, it can be carried forward up to seven years to offset income of those years.

It is important that an artist be familiar with the general compliance requirements of the Income Tax Act. The most important requirement is paying tax in quarterly installments. Generally, a self-employed individual is required to pre-pay his or her estimated tax liability in equal quarterly installments.

b. INCOME TAX AND THE ART DEALER

MW: Let's turn to dealers. Are there any tax features unique to them?

MB: Not really. Whether dealers operate as an unincorporated entity (sole proprietorship or partnership), or as a corporation, they are subject to all the rules and regulations applicable to a commercial enterprise for tax purposes. Like every other business, dealers must value the unsold works owned by the business, and defer those costs until such works are sold. Inventory valuation for a business is normally at the "lower of cost or market value." For tax purposes, a gallery's inventory includes works owned by the gallery, not works held on consignment.

MW: Can you touch on the unincorporated versus the corporate option of operating?

MB: The big advantage of a corporate set-up is that it gives the proprietor limited liability. Furthermore, depending on how much income the corporation generates from Canadian sources, it may be able to take advantage of the lower rate of corporate taxes — but only as long as the income remains in the company. If the owner requires all the earnings generated, he or she will have to pay tax personally on the money withdrawn from the corporation. Given the risks involved in running a gallery, the corporate form of organization is attractive. As well, a corporation may provide estate and tax planning benefits that might not otherwise be available to a sole proprietor.

MW: In nearly every case, a dealer is also a collector. Some collect mainly works by artists they represent, while others also collect the works of other artists. In addition, many artists keep some of their own work as a personal collection and often trade work with other artists, thereby developing personal collections. Does this raise any tax implications?

MB: The first one that springs to mind is the question of value. All transfers between related persons, other than spouses, must take place at fair market value for tax purposes. For instance, a recently acquired work can be transferred at cost from a gallery to the owner's personal collection because in this instance it may be assumed the cost of the work equals its fair market value. If the gallery has owned the work for some time and it has appreciated in value during that period, however, it would be difficult to argue that the fair market value equalled the original cost.

If a transfer is made from the personal collection to the gallery, the transferor may be able to argue that any gain realized should be treated as a capital gain. However, Revenue Canada may consider the collector to be acting as a trader and as a result deny the capital gains treatment. Each case would be determined on its own merits.

Another question that arises is how to record the transaction. If the work has originally been acquired by and for the gallery, then the simplest method of recording the transaction is to produce a normal invoice at the determined fair market value. If the dealer wishes to acquire works held on consignment from the artist, the transfer value should be the amount that would be paid by a third party to acquire the art after the most favored client discount.

c. INCOME TAX AND THE COLLECTOR

MW: Collectors may be individuals, unincorporated businesses, or corporations. Are there any tax differences between them?

MB: A distinction needs to be made between the private individual who collects art for personal enjoyment and the operating business that maintains an art collection as an adjunct to its normal operations. There are no immediate tax benefits or costs for the individual collector. The operating business, on the other hand, may be able to deduct certain costs relating to the ownership and maintenance of the art. For a cost or expense to be deductible, however, it must be laid out to earn income. The business must, therefore, be able to substantiate that the cost was incurred to earn income. This might be the case where a business displays art throughout the premises for the use and enjoyment of both staff and clients. It should be noted, however, that another restriction on the deductibility of costs and expenses is their reasonableness. The cost of a work of art must be reasonable in relation to its purpose in the business.

MW: What are the main tax implications for collectors?

MB: Tax implications arise on the disposition of part or all of an art collection. In general, if the collector sells a work, any gain or loss will be treated as a capital gain or loss and three-quarters of the gain realized would be included in income in the year of disposition.

In the case of the business collector, a disposition by sale will also be subject to the provisions of recapture of previously claimed capital cost allowance (CCA). If the entire collection were sold, then the depreciation claimed in past years would be subject to recapture and would be 100% taxable in the year of disposition. In most cases, only a portion of the collection is sold. Recapture is effected by reducing the then undepreciated capital cost of the collection — that is, the recapture will be realized through reduced future CCA claims.

189

d. INCOME TAX AND DONATIONS

MW: What are the tax implications of donating works of art?

MB: The tax treatment of donations varies depending on the nature of the property, the donor of the property, and the recipient of the donation. A corporation is entitled to deduct charitable donations from its income; individuals are entitled to a reduction in taxes payable.

The most generous tax treatment is afforded to gifts of Canadian cultural property. Artists or collectors donating property to a designated institution will be entitled to a tax credit based on the fair market value of the property at the time of the donation. Proceeds of the disposition are nil and, therefore, are not considered income.

Donations to Her Majesty or to charitable organizations of property that is not Canadian cultural property also result in a tax credit or tax deduction, depending on the donor. However, such a donation may also trigger a taxable event to the donor. Unlike gifts of Canadian cultural property, a gift of any other object results in a disposition equal to the amount elected by the donor as the value of the gift. In fact, the donor can elect that the proceeds on disposal be less, but not more, than the fair market value of the property. The most appropriate amount to elect should be determined on a case-by-case basis depending on the specific circumstances.

MW: No discussion of income taxes is complete without some comment on the rules related to Registered Retirement Savings Plans (RRSPs). What, if anything, is important for artists to know?

MB: Rather than going into all the rules associated with RRSPs (good reference materials are readily available from brokers, banks, and other financial institutions), I would like to address the carry-forward rules.

If a taxpayer fails to make an RRSP contribution before March 1 of the year following that in which the contribution was deductible, he or she can carry forward the deductibility entitlement for a limited number of years (determined by a fairly complex formula which usually works out close to the maximum of seven). In other words, if an artist's income makes him or her eligible for an RRSP deduction, but cash flow precludes a contribution, he or she can carry that eligibility forward for up to seven years during which time cash flow may improve. This change is advantageous for all taxpayers who have large year-to-year income fluctuations.

MW: That certainly can be the case for many artists. For that same reason, artists should be aware of the advantages of a "self-directed" RRSP through which he or she can ensure that investments in the plan are made with an eye to liquidity to cover a future need to withdraw some funds.

e. INCOME TAX AND ESTATE PLANNING

MW: When an individual dies there is a "deemed disposition" at the then "fair market value" of all the deceased's assets, and that valuation can trigger either capital gains tax or income tax or both. Does this apply to artists?

MB: The following comments apply to any taxpayer, including artists, dealers, and collectors. To examine the tax implications arising on the death of a taxpayer, we should first make the distinction between a "capital" asset and a "non-capital" asset. A work of art would be a "non-capital" asset for the artist who created it and for the dealer who carries it in his or her business inventory. An artwork would be a "capital" asset for a collector who owns it and maintains it within his or her collection.

MW: What are the rules for capital assets?

MB: At the date of death, there is an evaluation of all capital assets owned by the deceased to establish their fair market value. The results of this evaluation is called a "deemed disposition." It establishes the taxable capital gain or loss of the estate and must be reported on the final personal tax return prepared for the deceased.

One important exception to this rule is when capital property transfers by will to the spouse of the deceased. In this case the property transfers at the cost base — how much the property originally cost to make or produce — and as a result no gain is triggered at that time. However, if it's advantageous, the deceased's representatives can elect to transfer property at fair market value. For example, this option might be selected if the deceased has a capital loss carry-forward.

When capital property does not transfer to a spouse, care should be taken in calculating fair market value. The valuator should take into account legitimate deductions such as commissions payable on sales and the market value effect of a major body of work coming on the market at one time. The person responsible for the valuation could substantiate a discount from the "apparent" market value of works based on these factors.

MW: What about the effect on non-capital assets such as an artist's inventory of unsold works?

MB: Non-capital assets, such as business inventories, are valued on the same basis as they were valued up to the date of death. However, if the deceased artist, for example, had elected nil value for completed unsold works, there are a couple of special rules. Inventory items previously valued at nil value will now be valued at current fair market value. The inventory can then be reported in several different ways.

An effective option is based on the "rights and things" provisions of the Income Tax Act. Inventory value is not included in calculating income on the deceased's return. Inventory (artwork) is then distributed to beneficiaries within a specified time limit, and consequently a separate return is not needed. Because the value of the inventory is not used in calculating the deceased's return, its value may be considered as nil. Proceeds from eventual sales of the artwork, however, will be considered as taxable income for the beneficiaries in the year in which the artwork is sold. Moreover, no deduction will be available against the full proceeds, as the works would still be valued at the nil value reflected in the final tax return of the deceased artist.

Where a deceased taxpayer's representatives select either of the two other options, the artworks will then become "capital" assets of the beneficiaries. The cost base attributed to the value is included in income on the deceased's final tax return. This means that on ultimate sale, the difference between the proceeds of sale and the attributed capital cost of the work will be reported as a capital gain or loss of the beneficiary and taxed accordingly. The artworks remain non-capital assets and the total proceeds from sales will be subject to income tax in the year of sale, in the hands of the beneficiary receiving the proceeds.

Second, it can be considered as income in the tax return filed for the period to the date of death. This option results in the inventory value being added to the deceased's income otherwise calculated and taxed at the

193

marginal tax rate. This option taxes the value of the inventory at the deceased's highest effective tax rate.

Third, the deceased's legal representatives can elect not to include the inventory value in calculating income on the deceased taxpayer's final return. Instead, the inventory is reported in a separate return to be filed by the executors to reflect the valuation of the inventory at fair market value. In a certain sense this is a form of income splitting — except that the income is not being split between living persons to reduce tax rates, but between the deceased and a tax return prepared by the deceased's executors. This option allows reclaiming personal exemptions and the calculation of taxes using the full range of the graduated tax rates.

MW: Off the top of my head I'd say that the first option mentioned above provides the best solution.

MB: Not necessarily. I can think of several scenarios where the other options could be more advantageous. For instance, if the final tax return for the deceased indicated a net loss for the period and the inventory valuation could be substantiated at a value that would not create significant income, it could be beneficial to declare that value and take advantage of the loss to reduce the net taxable income. If the resulting tax were a reasonable amount, then the other two options would allow the artworks to be transferred to the beneficiaries as capital assets with attributed cost of the declared value. Future sales would then generate capital gains or losses subject to the favorable tax treatment available.

In every case, all three of the options should be reviewed to determine the maximum tax benefits considering both immediate taxes payable and those ultimately payable as the works are sold. It is important that the executors seek advice on this issue from an accountant or tax specialist.

MW: It seems that a successful artist would be well advised to get expert advice on estate planning while still alive.

MB: That's right, but that applies equally to any successful individual. One way the artist can ensure that this future tax liability is minimized or eliminated is to see that his or her will gives the power to the trustees to donate a portion of the unsold works (assuming this is in keeping with the artist's overall wishes). This procedure applies equally to collectors whose collection valuation at death could otherwise attract hefty taxes. If the work donated qualifies as Canadian Cultural Property, the deceased's estate is not required to recognize the proceeds of the donation on the final tax return of the artist but is, however, entitled to a charitable donation deduction or tax credit for the fair market value of the work donated. Of course, executors should also be given the power to sell works to meet outstanding debts and taxes owing on death in addition to having the power to gift works.

f. THE GOODS AND SERVICES TAX

MW: I understand that artworks are subject to the goods and services tax (GST). Does every sale of an artwork attract this tax?

GS: Since January 1, 1991 all sales of artworks in Canada have been subject to the GST where the sale is made by a GST registrant.

A few terms to understand in a discussion of the GST are "registrant" or "registered" and "supply" or "supplier." A registrant or registered business is any business that is required, or elects, to register with Revenue Canada as an agent to collect GST.

Supply or supplier refers to the provision of goods and/or services in the course of business that are normally recorded on an invoice rendered by the supplier to the recipient of the goods or services. In some cases, the evidence could be a receipt issued by the recipient to the supplier, as when artwork is donated, for example.

MW: Is everyone who sells art required to register for the GST?

GS: No. Individuals, corporations, partnerships, etc., are only required to register if they are carrying on "commercial activities" in Canada. The definition of commercial activities is rather broad, but it is commonly understood that any individual or corporation engaged in a business must register for GST purposes. Individuals who carry on a business without a "reasonable expectation of profit" are specifically prohibited from registering. Most artists who rely on the sale of their work by itself or in conjunction with some other form of commercial activity will be required to register for GST purposes and collect the tax on all their revenues. Artists who engage in painting, etc. as a hobby and sell only the occasional work are not allowed to register for GST purposes.

Art dealers are required to register for GST and collect the tax on their revenues. Individual collectors, on the other hand, are not permitted to register for GST purposes, because collecting is not a commercial activity undertaken with a reasonable expectation of profit. However, a business that collects art as an adjunct to its business operations is already registered for GST because of its primary operations, and therefore can take advantage of the input tax credits (ITCs) discussed below.

MW: On what revenues typically associated with art would a registrant be required to collect GST?

GS: Virtually all revenues earned by a GST registrant in its art business are subject to GST. These include sales, leasing of works, services (including teaching, framing, etc.), and sales of equipment or supplies.

Revenues that are not subject to GST include earnings as an employee, investment income, grants and awards, and proceeds of sales of works of art exported by the registrant from Canada.

MW: I have heard some artists refer to themselves as a "small supplier." They told me they do not have to charge GST on the sale of their work. Is this true?

GS: Yes. GST legislation includes a provision that very small businesses are not required to register for GST purposes even if they are carrying on commercial activities — specifically, individuals or other persons with otherwise GST-taxable revenues (i.e., gross revenues) of $30 000 or less per year. Such persons are known as "small suppliers." Any person underneath the $30 000 threshold may elect to register voluntarily. Once an election is made it remains in effect for the whole of that taxation year and GST must then be collected on all taxable revenues. The election may, however, be rescinded subsequently, but only if notice is given before the start of the next taxation year.

Remember that the gross revenue threshold includes all forms of GST taxable revenues. For example, an artist could have annual sales of artwork of $20 000. In order to supplement that income, he or she works part time as a retail clerk for a clothing store earning $20 000 per year. As the clothing store wages are excluded from GST taxable revenues, the artist still qualifies as a small supplier for GST purposes. If however, the artist supplemented income by doing, say, home renovations on a self-employed contract basis grossing $20 000 per year, then his or her combined annual revenues would be over the $30 000 threshold and he or she would be required to register and charge GST on both the sales of artwork and the home renovations.

MW: What factors would influence the small supplier's decision to register?

GS: First, GST registrants are required to collect GST on all taxable revenues. This raises the cost of the artwork, or other service, being provided to the purchaser. If the purchaser itself is a business, then the GST paid to acquire the supply may be refundable. Such refunds to purchasers are known as input tax credits (ITCs). If, however, the majority of an artist's clients are not GST registrants, and are therefore not eligible for a refund of GST paid, then it might make sense for the artist not to register for GST purposes. In this way the artist avoids having to charge customers who would have to bear the full burden of the tax. Small suppliers who choose to register for the GST make themselves eligible for ITCs for GST paid on most of their business expenditures.

Any small art business whose customers are predominantly GST registrants may prefer to become a GST registrant and thus allow its clients to claim ITCs.

MW: I suppose that some artists may decide to remain a non-registrant simply to avoid the hassle of the paperwork associated with being a registrant. What exactly must a registrant do to satisfy the reporting requirements of Revenue Canada?

GS: Registrants are required to file a periodic return with Revenue Canada. In this return, the registrant reports all of his or her revenues and the GST collected. On the same return, the registrant makes a claim for ITCs. The registrant is required to send a cheque to Revenue Canada for the difference between GST collected and the ITC claim. If the ITC claim exceeds the GST collected, the government will refund the difference. The frequency of filing returns varies with the total GST taxable gross revenue of the registrant.

MW: What about the application of GST to art imported into Canada? I understand that in some cases, an importer has to pay GST when art is imported, and in other cases, the art can be imported without paying GST. Can you explain this to me?

GS: As GST is a tax on consumption in Canada, it makes sense that imports into Canada would be subject to GST. In fact, the importer of art generally has to pay GST on the imported value of the goods at the time of importation. If the importer deals through a customs broker, the GST would be payable to the broker. If the importer does not have a customs broker, the GST is generally payable to Revenue Canada at the border prior to the art being released to the importer.

Art can be imported free of GST in certain circumstances. Specifically, an artwork qualifies for non-taxable importation if three conditions are met: where the work is part of a shipment of imported art on consignment and the total value of the shipment is at least $250 000, and at the time of importation it is reasonable to expect that at least 75% in value of the shipment will be exported within one year after importation, and the work is imported for the purpose of supply by the importer in the ordinary course of the importer's business. If all of these criteria are not met, then GST will apply at the time of importation of the artwork.

Of course, if the importer is a GST registrant, he or she would normally be eligible for an ITC for the imported goods, claimable on the next GST return. When imported works of art are sold in Canada, GST must be collected on the sale and remitted by the vendor.

MW: And what about gifting a work of art? Does GST need to be remitted?

GS: GST does not need to be remitted on a gift between arms-length parties. This applies even if the person making the gift is a GST registrant. In the case of a gift between persons not dealing at arm's length — family members for example — when the donor is a registrant, then GST should be remitted on the fair market value of the gift.

MW: Suppose that last year I was a bit short of cash when it came time to pay my accountant so I gave him a painting instead. Should I be concerned about GST?

GS: Yes. Barter transactions do not escape the GST. As a registrant, it is your responsibility to collect GST on all taxable supplies you have exchanged for cash or for goods or services. In this case, you have supplied your accountant with a painting and he has supplied you with accounting services. You are responsible for remitting GST for the painting.

CONTRIBUTORS

Stephen B. Smart is a partner of the law firm Osler, Hoskin & Harcourt (Toronto). Mr. Smart has had a long association with the field of visual arts in Canada and has acted for a number of well-known artists, dealers, and collectors. He has been on the Board of Directors of the Ontario Craft Council, was the founding chair of the Friends of the Ontario College of Art Inc., has served on the acquisitions committee of international contemporary art at the Art Gallery of Ontario, has served as a member and vice chair of the City of Toronto Public Art Commission, is a past chair of The Corporate Art Collectors Group, and is currently on the Board of Directors of The Studio, a project to develop a retirement home for artists in need. Mr. Smart played a significant role in collecting the well-known corporate collection of contemporary Canadian art at Osler, Hoskin & Harcourt. In 1993, he was the co-curator of an exhibition of contemporary Canadian art that travelled to South Korea as part of Expo '93.

Mary Baxter resides in Owen Sound, Ontario where she is a writer, poet, and commentator on cultural issues. She has also been active in the administrative area of the visual arts.

Eve Baxter is a well-known art consultant who has been involved in a number of ground-breaking public art projects in Canada. She has also been involved with the development of numerous corporate art collections across Canada. She has worked as both a professional and volunteer in the arts in Canada for over 40 years.

Glen A. Bloom, an expert in copyright and trademark law, heads the Intellectual Property Department of the Ottawa offices of the law firm Osler, Hoskin & Harcourt, at which he is a partner. He has a keen interest in issues related to visual arts and has been a regular contributor and speaker on these issues for the Canadian Museums Association and for other organizations. He is a lecturer in intellectual property law at the Faculty of Law, University of Ottawa and a member of the Board of Directors of the Ottawa Arts Centre Foundation. He is a past president of the Ottawa School of Art and has served as a member of the City of Ottawa's Visual Arts Advisory Committee.

Brian Blugerman was educated at the University of Toronto where he received a B.A. in philosophy and later a law degree. Mr. Blugerman practises with the Toronto office of Osler, Hoskin & Harcourt specializing in the media and entertainment law fields. Prior to becoming a lawyer, Mr. Blugerman worked as a pianist and songwriter in Los Angeles and New York.

Jeffrey Spalding is an artist, educator, and curator. He has taught art and art history at colleges and universities in Canada for the past 15 years and has published an array of articles, catalogues, and monographs. Previously he was the curator of the Glenbow Museum and the Art Gallery of Nova Scotia. He has been Director of the University of Lethbridge Art Gallery since 1981. In 1993 he was awarded the Board of Governors Award of Excellence by the Alberta College of Art for outstanding contributions to the arts in Alberta.

Malcolm Welch is a retired businessman and chartered accountant who is well versed in the accounting and tax issues related to the field of visual arts. For many years, Mr. Welch owned and operated The Welch Gallery in the Ottawa area. He has been a passionate collector of contemporary art and a great supporter of a number of well-known artists at work today. For his contribution to this book, Mr. Welch interviewed two tax partners from Welch & Company in Ottawa, **Michael Burch** and **Garth Steele.**